GAY VEGAS

GAY VEGAS

A GUIDE TO
THE OTHER SIDE OF SIN CITY

STEVE FRIESS

HUNTINGTON PRESS
LAS VEGAS, NEVADA

GAY VEGAS
A GUIDE TO THE OTHER SIDE OF SIN CITY

Published by
Huntington Press
3665 S. Procyon Ave.
Las Vegas, Nevada 89103
telephone: (702) 252-0655
facsimile: (702) 252-0675
email: books@huntingtonpress.com

ISBN: 978-0-929712-46-8

Cover photo: Tomas Muscionico
Author photo: Denise Truscello
Design & production: Laurie Shaw

Photo credits: Photos courtesy of the *Las Vegas Review-Journal*: pg. 2; MGM Mirage, pgs. 14, 15, 18, 25, 36, 40, 43, 60, 61, 62, 66, 71, 73, 78, 81, 84, 91, 127, 129, 138, 141, 146, 149; Cirque Du Soleil, pgs. 92, 104, 113, 129; Harrah's Entertainmnt, pgs. 20, 32, 68, 69, 90, 94, 99, 106, 107, 111, 112, 126, 148, 151, 154; General Growth Properties Inc., pgs. 142, 152; *Phantom: The Las Vegas Spectacular*, pg. 93; Paramount Parks, pg. 35; Las Vegas Hilton, pg. 105; Dennis McBride's collection, pgs. 5, 184, 187, 190; Susan Feninger, pg. 86; Wynn Resort Ltd., pgs. 21, 67, 102, 103, 150, 156, 172; Krāve, pg. 123; Ron DeCar, pg. 173; Tao, pg. 64; Golden Rainbow, pg. 197; First Friday pg. 171; Venetian Las Vegas, pgs. 101, 161; Liberace Museum, pg. 163; Christopher Allegra, pg. 56; Roger Thomas, pg. 28; Iris Dumak, pg. 22; Blue Moon Resort, pg. 55; Wayne Bernath, pgs. 41, 44, 97; AFAN, pgs. 183, 197. All other photos shot by Steve Friess.

DEDICATION

To Miles,
You're all the gay Vegas I'll ever need.

ACKNOWLEDGMENTS

The same mid-July week I received the advance for this book from Huntington Press, the temperature in Las Vegas soared to a high of 117. The poor much-abused air conditioner on our house just couldn't take it anymore and at 1 a.m., my partner woke me drenched in sweat to announce its demise. As we gathered our puppies, Black and Jack, and went to stay first at a Motel 6 and then, for two nights, on a futon at the home of our friends Walt Herron and Terry Wilsey, all I could think of was how much a new A/C was going to cost. When I finally found out, I said to my partner, "Well, I guess this means I really have to write this thing now."

There were many times in the subsequent year that Miles wondered whether I'd actually do it. "How's that gay guidebook coming?" went from an amusing catch-phrase around our home to an annoyance and, on days when I'd take on new freelance assignments after vowing to turn my attention to the book, a gentle accusation.

Well, looky here. The thing got done. And nobody is more surprised than I am. Miles sure isn't; he always knew it would, but hoped he might encourage me to avoid the mad rush that accompanied the last six weeks of the project. Which should be a lesson to him, as if he didn't know it before: Time management isn't my strong suit. But somehow, despite all those afternoons when I was supposed to be writing and instead I was playing Scrabble on the Internet, the work always seems to get finished.

Many people helped. Walt and Terry, our adopted fairy grand-parents, provided many suppers, many ideas, and many good laughs. Terry, the gayest travel agent in all of Vegas (702/731-2114), frequently and flexibly took my calls as I tried to figure out what belonged in here and what didn't. And Dr. Herron, a one-time Man of the Year through the Gay and Lesbian Community Center, has, in his dotage, reminded me that being gay is a lifelong experience and not, as the popular media and culture would have us believe, merely a phenomenon of the young.

My family, of course, has always loved me for who I am, and that has empowered me throughout my life. To my father and mother, Neil and Joan Friess, my sisters and their husbands, Sheryl and David Zellis, and Elynne and Tom Arleo, my aunts and uncles, Susan and Richard, Kenny and Robin, I am grateful. Their children—Zach, Courtney, Siona, Arielle, Daniel, Chaim, Garrett, Nicky, Allyson, Matt, Elizabeth, and Heather—have been raised to understand that being gay does not diminish a person's value, a fact that should encourage all of us that the future for people who are different will continue to improve. And my grandparents, Claire and Doug Martin and Morris and Claire Friess, all rolled with the times after I revealed my true self to them.

It pains me more than I can say that I finally wrote a book and my beloved Grandma Grandma isn't alive to see it. She was, after all, the one who told me presciently back in 1997, "I think you'll stay in Vegas a long time. It seems to suit you." I was dismissive; she knew.

In Las Vegas, I have many friends and mentors. None more sig-nificant to me, though, than Jamie Koch, a boy I met when he was six and who is growing up, astonishingly, into a man, while the rest of us don't ever seem to age at all. I joined Big Brothers Big Sisters of Nevada in 1997 to be an inspiration to a kid in need; Jamie's good nature and good humor and his complete and easy-going acceptance have taught me, comforted me, made me effusively proud. Stacey, Billie, and Henry, you've done well.

The first gay Las Vegan I knew is now at the *Arizona Republic*, but without Shaun McKinnon I wouldn't have ever conceived of visiting, much less moving to, a place like this. Others who helped in ways obvious and less obvious include *Las Vegas Nightbeat* publisher Bill Schafer, *QVegas* publisher Kelly MacFarlane-Smith and editor Chris Campbell, Clark Wolf, Frank Marino, Joey Arias, John McCoy, Paul Speirs, Ron DeCar, Candice Nichols, Rob Schlegel, Jack Levine, Homer Marrs, Erica Grimaldo, Jon Afalla, and Mike Spadoni. Other straight-ally colleagues who need mention include Adam Goldman, Jon Ralston, Norm Clarke, John Katsamiletes, John L. Smith, Jane Ann Morrison, Jimmy Diggs, Mark Vavrick, Beth Fisher, Kendall Tenney, Emily Richmond, Molly Ball, Mitch Fox, Steve Sebelius, Dave Berns, and Natalie Patton.

Obviously, I'm grateful to Anthony Curtis, Deke Castleman, Laurie Shaw, and Bethany Coffey at Huntington Press for heckling me to get the proposal and then the book finished. I'm sure they had their doubts. And a thank you to Tomas Muscionico for the cover photo and Denise Truscello for my author photo.

And thanks to those editors and producers around the nation who have kept me working and paying my bills while I worked on this project: Dennis Kelly at *USA Today*, Camille Hunt and Glenn Albin at *Vegas*, David Jefferson and Bret Begun at *Newsweek*, Darren Frei at *Out Traveler*, Evan Hansen at *Wired*, Joan Nassivera at the *New York Times*, and Dana Dickey and Irene Schneider at *Condé Nast Traveler*.

Through my nearly 15-year involvement with the National Lesbian and Gay Journalists Association, I've been inspired by dozens of people who have helped me produce this and many other works. Among them are Bob Witeck, Jim Harper, Steve Rothaus, Ric Katz, Geoff Dankert, Bryan Weakland, Randy Dotinga, Chris Badowski, Jason Howe, David Steinberg, Rose Arce, Mike Wilke, Pamela Strother, Eric Hegedus, and, of course, the late dear NLGJA founder Roy Aarons. And other friends across the nation whom I owe props to include Lyzette Austen, Melissa Bernardoni, Sue Ponsford, Craig Nesler, Nell Minow, and David Elias.

Back in the day when I was a full-time staffer at the *Las Vegas Review-Journal*, I joined my colleagues' disdain for PR folks as a matter of professional obligation. But since becoming a freelance writer, I've discovered that they are vital to helping me know what's new and accessing the people I need to speak to. And over the years they've taken my calls seeking niggling details I should already have had in my notes or complaining about some problem someone was giving me. They've also been good sports about understanding that criticism I write is always heartfelt and balanced, never mean-spirited and personal, part of the job. So, in no particular order, thanks go out to Dave Kirvin and Bill Doak and their teams at Kirvin-Doak; Alan Feldman, Jenn Michaels, and the MGM Mirage bunch; Erica Yowell at the LVCVA; Dawn Christensen, formerly of Harrah's; Alberto Lopez and the Harrah's team; Denise Randazzo, Ruth Furman, Wayne Bernath, Ira Sternberg, Meryl Scheinman, Lori Nelson, Candi Cazau, and Ron Reese. And some forward-thinking gaming executives and leaders helped transform this city, including Jan Jones, Felix Rappaport, Terry Lanni, David Parks, Danny Greenspun, Steve and Elaine Wynn, Bob Forbuss, George Maloof, and Terry Jicinsky.

Finally, a few folks held my hand and led me out of the valley of misery following the devastation that struck me in October 2002. Kelly Schwarz, Trevor Price, Tony Plohetski, and David Pohl, your support and patience made all the difference.

Fortunately, since Miles came along I haven't needed one so much. After two years of my bumping about in the wilderness, he found me and he loved me, nosepicking and all. He gave my life meaning, direction, humor, and happiness. For that, as Nicky would sing in the brilliant and, sadly for Vegas, short-lived *Avenue Q*, I shout "Hooray!"

I love you, bunny.

Steve Friess
Las Vegas, Nevada
May 1, 2007

CONTENTS

Maps are located on pages: 47; 48-49; 50; 119; 169;
180-181

INTRODUCTION

For the past year, virtually every time I told a friend I was working on a gay guidebook to Las Vegas, the sarcastic response was a variation of: *"Boy, that'll be a short book."*

Har har. Funny, yes. But true? Not anymore.

Certainly, what you're holding in your hands would have been just a pamphlet back when I first moved to Las Vegas in 1996 to work at the *Las Vegas Review-Journal*. But like everything else in a city that's growing at a dizzying pace, a decade has meant a radical change for everyone in this valley, including gay, lesbian, bisexual, and transgender (GLBT) residents and visitors.

Consider the difference. Back then, the shows on the Strip were, largely, aggressively heterosexual, from girlie productions to homophobic comedians. There was little to get excited about in the way of shopping, fine dining, or culture. The newspaper I arrived to work at had, only a few years earlier, refused to run a comic strip because a teenaged character had come out of the closet. A same-sex couple who wanted to marry anywhere in this town, which ironically purports to celebrate sin and liberation, would have been laughed out the door.

Today, the desert oasis founded by Mormon missionaries has blossomed as a mecca for gays. Most of the major hotel-casinos allow same-sex unions in their chapels, even though the Nevada electorate passed a constitutional amendment banning gay marriage in 2002. Two recent chairmen of the Las Vegas Chamber of Commerce were openly gay, as was, until recently, the county manager, who was promoted to a top post within Harrah's Entertainment. The mayor is gin-swilling Oscar Goodman, a man so publicly pro-gay he showed up in drag at the debut of a new, though short-lived, gay club in 2005. Goodman also appeared in a hilarious queer version of *A Christmas Carol* as one half of a gay couple—the state's ACLU executive director was his paramour—in 2003.

The Strip, it seems, has seen the light. Such hotels as New York-New York, Luxor, Paris, and Wynn Las Vegas all advertise heavily in gay publications. The Las Vegas Convention and Visitors Authority had a float in New York City's Gay Pride Parade in June 2006 for the first time, complete with showgirls and beefcake imported to Manhattan from major Strip shows for the occasion. This year, Paris Las Vegas was a finalist for a GLAAD Media Award for the hotel's gay-targeted advertising campaign. In addition, the Human Rights Campaign launched a nationwide fundraising concert tour here starring a list of gay music icons, including Erasure, Cyndi Lauper and Debbie Harry. And much of this is happening because a 2005 study by Community

Marketing Inc. showed that Las Vegas was the second most popular destination for gay male travelers after New York. That's right; more gays come here than go to San Francisco. Believe it or not.

Consider that the world's two largest gaming companies, MGM Mirage and Harrah's, offer their employees same-sex domestic-partnership benefits, give thousands of dollars to GLBT and HIV/AIDS causes, have high-level openly gay executives, and spar for bragging rights over who has the better gay-positive rating from the Human Rights Campaign. When a gay Wynn Las Vegas marketing representative heard that I was writing a piece on gay Vegas for *Out Traveler* magazine in 2005, he e-mailed to urge consideration of the new $2.7 billion property, noting exuberantly, "The Wynn is the gayest hotel in Las Vegas!" It's hard to imagine Bugsy Siegel's boys doing something like that.

In addition, Las Vegas is now a food capital of the United States, rivaling New York and San Francisco with vaunted chefs like Joël Robuchon, Mario Batali, Bobby Flay, Susan Feniger, Guy Savoy, Alessandro Stratta, and Wolfgang Puck. Bellagio and the Venetian display the finest of fine art in galleries. Fifth Avenue, Rodeo Drive, and North Michigan Avenue pale in comparison to the stores you'll find at the Bellagio, Wynn, Venetian, Planet Hollywood, and Fashion Show malls.

And the shows? Elton John, *Zumanity, Mamma Mia!,* and *Le Rêve* couldn't be more queer, and gay subtexts pop up where you'd least expect them, as when the team of hunky men writhe all over one another in Celine Dion's *A New Day* .... A recent migration of Broadway to the Strip has been a mixed bag, with *Hairspray* and *Avenue Q* both fizzling quickly, with a Vegas-ized *Phantom of the Opera* at the Venetian looking to stick around for a while and the jury still out on *The Producers* at Paris. And some old favorites endure, including the campy *Jubilee!* and *An Evening at La Cage.*

Oddly, while the tourist corridor has embraced the pink dollar and life for GLBT people continues to improve in the valley, the gay scene itself remains stuck in neutral. Las Vegas has about the same number of gay bars now as a decade ago. The total annual budget for

The Center, our GLBT hub, is only $200,000. The Gay Pride Parade is an embarrassment, unsupported and sparsely attended as it is by the community at large.

There's also no Boystown or Castro, no gay ghetto in Las Vegas. Of course, we also don't have a Chinatown, unless you count the series of Asian-themed strip malls that line Spring Mountain Road. In that way, Vegas is something of an archetype for future American cities: fully integrated, fully assimilated. Other than a lingering African-American ghetto known as West Side, we don't have sections of town denoted by minority; we're separated by income and class, which does tend to skew in certain directions for certain groups.

But gay people here don't feel the need to band together in certain geographic areas. Why not? Because from Summerlin to Anthem, from Boulder City to Mount Charleston, we are everywhere and, if not always embraced, we're largely tolerated.

Still, that lack of a center of gravity leaves a GLBT community that fails to gather its political, financial, and cultural strength when threats—such as the insidious anti-marriage amendment that passed in 2002—emerge.

Sadly, too, there may be a lot for gay men to do in Vegas, but the city offers pathetic little for lesbians, which is why this book is so deficient in information for women. There are, I was shocked to discover, simply no dyke bars in Las Vegas and just a few lesbian groups. In most bars, lesbians are welcome and, as The Center's executive director Candice Nichols explains on page 193, our gay male and lesbian populations are unusually integrated. Still, it's a glaring omission.

All that said, GLBT people continue to flock here, along with the rest of the world, because we've got great weather, plenty of jobs, and low taxes. In this guidebook, you'll learn what to do, where to go, what you must see and taste. And you'll meet a number of GLBT entrepreneurs and leaders who have made this city what it is today.

As the flight attendants often say when flights land at McCarran International Airport—and only when they land *here*—good luck.

GENERAL INFORMATION

ORIENTATION

About 1.6 million people live in the Las Vegas region, including about 575,000 people within the Las Vegas city limits. Henderson, North Las Vegas, and Boulder City are also nearby municipalities included in the metropolitan area, and Clark is the county that contains all of them. Las Vegas is the largest American city founded in the 20th century and continues to grow by about 5,000 new residents per month on balance.

"Las Vegas" as it's known is comprised of two significant tourist areas, the Strip and downtown. The Strip refers, technically, to a four-mile stretch of Las Vegas Boulevard South in unincorporated Clark County from Sahara Avenue to Russell Road. However, casinos and hotels along Paradise Road, Harmon Avenue, Flamingo Road, and Tropicana Avenue within a mile of Las Vegas Boulevard are also usually included in the common designation, the "Strip corridor." Downtown refers to a cluster of older less opulent hotel-casinos within a mile's radius of the region's first paved street, Fremont Street. These properties, known collectively as Glitter Gulch for the intense concentration of neon signs, tend to lack the grandeur and amenities of Strip resorts, but often offer good-value accommodations and gambling, sleeper restaurants, and the spectacular Fremont Street Experience light show.

GAY ORIENTATION

Las Vegas doesn't have a gay neighborhood or district the way that many other major tourist destinations do. There are, however, two main clusters of gay bars.

• **The Fruit Loop:** So named by gay developers for the strange circuitous traffic pattern of the area, the Fruit Loop is found along Paradise Road about a quarter-mile south of Harmon Avenue and one mile east of the Strip. The key businesses here include Get Booked, The Buffalo, Gipsy, 8½, and Free Zone.

• **Commercial Center:** A large shopping center laid out as a square on Sahara Avenue about a mile east of the Strip, the key entities include the GLBT community center, the Spotlight Lounge, and two bathhouses.

Beyond this, one-off gay bars and businesses are scattered throughout the valley.

WHEN TO GO

These days, very few "quiet" periods appear on the Las Vegas calendar. Traditionally, visitor counts and room rates have been lowest during the span from just after Thanksgiving until Christmas and in the blistering months of July and August. But this is no longer the case. The National Finals Rodeo invades for about two weeks in early December, when tens of thousands of cowboys, cowgals, and country-and-western aficionados clog the place. And though the kid-friendly frenzy of the early 1990s has passed Las Vegas by, families still show up in droves during summer break. The one spell of the year that is guaranteed to be slow is the week immediately prior to Christmas Eve, after the rodeo gallops off and before the Christmas rush begins.

At any time of the year, hotel rates fluctuate radically. As a rule they're generally much less expensive Sunday through Thursday. To avoid coming during periods with major conventions, which inflate room rates and make dinner reservations and show tickets harder to come by, visit the Las Vegas Convention and Visitors Authority's convention calendar at www.lvcva.com/finder/conventioncalendar.

CLIMATE

While the word is that the desert is miserably hot, the truth is that's only true from June to early September, when the mercury climbs over 100 and sometimes stays there for weeks on end, often not dipping below 90, even in the early morning. For the most part, the rest of the year is temperate—it's usually in the 80s and 90s for much of September through mid-November and from March to June. High winter temperatures, from about mid-November through February, usually settle in at the 50s and 60s, dropping into the 30s and 40s at night. Snow happens, too, though it's treated as a fleeting and baffling special effect that usually melts within hours.

ATTIRE

The weather and the long-distance walking required on the Strip dictate that dress is casual in most instances. None of the top-end restaurants require a jacket or collared shirt—although a couple, including Picasso at Bellagio, encourage it—and people frequently show up for important conventions in jeans and gym shoes. Shorts and T-shirts are in season from March to November.

HISTORY

Anasazi and Paiute Native Americans had inhabited the Las Vegas Valley for centuries. Mormon missionaries built a fort here in 1855, but they abandoned the settlement three years later. Development began in earnest in 1905 when the San Pedro, Los Angeles and Salt Lake Railroad founded the town. Las Vegas was incorporated in 1911. Wide-open gambling was legalized and construction began on the Hoover Dam, both in 1931, which kicked off the modern era. The casinos and dam brought thousands to the valley to live and work.

The first Strip property, the El Rancho Vegas, was built in 1941 outside the city limits so that it could sprawl and avoid city regulations.

Bugsy Siegel opened the celebrated Flamingo in 1946, launching a resort boom that included the Desert Inn (1950), the Sands and Sahara (1952), the Dunes and Riviera (1955), the Tropicana (1957), and the Stardust (1958). The Rat Pack, a collection of iconic singers including Frank Sinatra, Dean Martin, and Sammy Davis Jr., loomed large on the entertainment scene in the 1950s and 1960s and Elvis Presley became an iconic Las Vegan in the 1970s.

The modern era of megaresorts was kicked off when Steve Wynn opened the Mirage in 1989. The next decade saw implosions of such Vegas institutions as the Sands and the Dunes to make way for Bellagio, the Venetian, Mandalay Bay, and, most recently, Wynn Las Vegas.

GAY HISTORY

Gay men and lesbians have had a steady and significant hand in making Las Vegas and Nevada what they are today. Tellingly, though, such showmen as Liberace and Siegfried and Roy, who were in their day synonymous with Las Vegas, never publicly acknowledged their gay sexual orientation. (Several others have attested to Siegfried Fischbacher and Roy Horn's having once been a couple, including Shirley MacLaine in a 1999 *Vanity Fair* article and MGM Mirage spokesman Alan Feldman following the 2003 on-stage tiger-mauling incident that

crippled Horn and ended their long-running illusionist act at the Mirage.)

Long before that, though, there was a group of gay enlistees for the Civilian Conservation Corps near Moapa in

1938. The Oscar Wilde film *The Picture of Dorian Gray* was shown in a theater in 1915. And a female impersonator performed at a popular Las Vegas restaurant, the Green Shack, in the 1930s, all according to research by gay historian Dennis McBride. The region's

first known gay bar, the Kit Kat Club, stood at Fremont and Charleston and even ran ads in local newspapers in the 1940s, and a gay paper called *Gay Notes From Le Café* was published in the 1970s, McBride says.

Sodomy was made illegal in Nevada in 1911 and remained so until the Legislature repealed the law in 1993, in large part thanks to the courageous activism of then-State Senator Lori Lippman-Brown. It was a remarkable year, as then-Governor Bob Miller, a moderate Democrat, campaigned for re-election by visiting a gay bar in the Reno area. In 1999, the Legislature made Nevada then the 11th state in the nation to pass ENDA, the Employment Non-Discrimination Act, which was authored by the state's first openly gay legislator, Assemblyman David Parks, and signed by Republican Governor Kenny Guinn.

Threatened by the prospect of legal same-sex marriage, conservative activist Richard Ziser authored a ballot initiative to ban gay nuptials in Nevada. It passed overwhelmingly in the successive general elections of 2000 and 2002, as was required by law to codify it in the state's constitution. Yet in subsequent years came two interesting and promising developments: the 2003 Legislature unanimously passed a measure giving funeral and hospital-visitation rights to same-sex partners and Ziser lost in a landslide in a 2004 bid to unseat U.S. Senator Harry Reid. In addition, such major Las Vegas employers as MGM Mirage, Harrah's, Greenspun Media Group, and Wynn Resorts extended health benefits to the partners of their gay and lesbian employees.

GETTING THERE

BY GROUND: Las Vegas is easily accessible from both Utah and Southern California via Interstate 15, from Reno via US 95 and from Phoenix via US 93. There's also a Greyhound bus terminal at 200 S. Main Street in downtown Las Vegas. Amtrak trains no longer service the city.

BY AIR: More than 40 airlines fly into McCarran International Airport, including direct international flights from Germany, Britain, South Korea, Mexico, Canada, and the Philippines. The two largest carriers serving the city are Southwest and US Air. McCarran International Airport is unusually close to the action for a major-city airport, just a mile from the Strip, and taxicabs are plentiful just outside the baggage-claim area. The airport was one of the first in the nation to provide free wireless Internet access and a 24-hour gym. Plus, if you forgot to buy souvenirs during your trip, most of the hotel conglomerates have shops there, too.

GETTING AROUND

BY TAXI: Cabs are plentiful at the airport, major hotel-casinos, and the Las Vegas Convention Center, but are a bit harder to find elsewhere. Two of the main cab companies are Yellow/Checker/Star (702/873-2000) and Lucky Cab Co. (702/477-7555).

BY RENTAL CAR: The $170 million McCarran Rent-A-Car Center, located three miles south of Las Vegas' McCarran International Airport, opened in spring 2007. The center consolidates 11 car-rental companies under one roof at 7135 Gilespie Street. Now, instead of renting cars at counters in the airport terminal, then waiting for the rental-car company's own shuttle bus as before, all customers board common-use shuttles run by the airport to move between the terminal and the rental-car center. (Rental-car companies rent 1.8 million cars at McCarran, the nation's sixth-busiest airport, every year.)

National chains include the usual suspects: Avis, Budget, Enterprise, Dollar, Hertz, Alamo/National, Payless, Advantage, Savmor, and Thrifty. One lesser-known regional chain that tends to have consistently lower prices is U.S. Rent-A-Car (800/777-9377; www.us-rentacar. com); it doesn't have a counter at the airport facility. Several companies also rent ultra-luxury vehicles, including Rent-A-Vette (800/372-1981; www.exoticcarrentalslasvegas.com) and Dream Car Rentals (877/373-2601; www.dreamcarrentals.com).

BY PRIVATE VEHICLE: Parking is free at almost every major hotel-casino on the Strip in surface lots and garages and usually free to hotel guests in garages in the downtown Las Vegas cluster of hotels. Furthermore, motorists can valet park almost everywhere for free unless the lots are full, although it's customary to tip the drivers a couple of dollars when they return your car to you.

BY BUS: The Citizens Area Transit (702/CAT-RIDE; www.rtcsouthern nevada.com/cat/) operates public bus service, including double-decker "Deuce" buses that roll up and down the Strip 24 hours a day. The cost is $2 each way on the Strip, $1.25 each way for off-Strip routes.

BY MONORAIL: The Las Vegas Monorail (www.lvmonorail. com) follows a four-mile route parallel to and east of the Strip that starts at the MGM Grand and ends at the Sahara hotel.

There are stops at Paris/Bally's, Flamingo, Harrah's/Imperial Palace, and the Las Vegas Hilton resorts, as well as the Las Vegas Convention Center. It costs $5 per ride, with multi-ride discounts available, and is open Mon.–Fri. 7 a.m.–2 a.m. and Fri.–Sun. 7 a.m.–3 a.m. Fair warning: The signage inside the monorail suggests stops are accessible to several other hotels. Any hotels not listed above are at least a half-mile walk from any monorail stop. Also, folks with Nevada ID can ride for $1 a ride but this option is only available at staffed windows and is not advertised anywhere. In addition, free privately operated trams ferry passengers between Treasure Island and the Mirage, as well as between Mandalay Bay, Luxor, and Excalibur.

MEDIA

The Las Vegas region is served by two daily mainstream newspapers, the *Las Vegas Review-Journal* (www.reviewjournal.com) and the *Las Vegas Sun* (www.lasvegassun.com), which have been distributed

QVIP CARD

It's actually financially worthwhile to be gay in Vegas, now that the folks at *QVegas* magazine have concocted this free saver card. The discounts available with it are far-ranging and include line-pass privileges at Krāve, 10 percent off meals at Toucan's, $2 off admission to the Atomic Testing Museum, $6 admission to the Bellagio Gallery of Fine Art, and more. More than 50 vendors participate. To get one, e-mail your name, address, phone number, and birthdate to vip@qvegas.com or visit www.qvegas.com/vip.

together since October 2005. The *R-J* is generally perceived as having a conservative-libertarian bias in its editorials; the libertarian faction of editorial board opined against banning same-sex marriage in 2002. For entertainment news, the Friday *R-J* carries the "Neon" section, which can also be found on the Web site, and regular e-mail updates are available by registering for free online.

The gay media consists of the monthlies *QVegas* (www.qvegas.com), *Out Las Vegas* (www.outlas vegas. com), and *Las Vegas Night Beat* (www. lvnightbeat.com). *QVegas* is a glossy magazine that appears at the beginning of each month, providing news and entertainment coverage. *Out Las Vegas* is a newsprint bar publication put out in the middle of each month by Stonewall Publishing, the same company that publishes *QVegas*. And the half-size magazine *Night Beat* also comes out at the beginning of the month and contains news and entertainment columns. It's owned by Bill Schafer, a former editor of the *Las Vegas Bugle*, which was bought out by Stonewall and renamed in 2004.

In addition, a national bimonthly glossy called *Envy Man* is published out of Las Vegas, is found for free at some gay establishments, and can be purchased at some newsstands. The magazine provides lifestyle articles and fashion spreads laden with plenty of male eye candy plucked from the Nevada-based Envy Model Talent's stable. Their Web site is www.envyman.com.

Plus, while not gay-focused, the weekly celebrity-interview podcast

"The Strip" is co-hosted by a gay couple—yours truly and my partner, Miles Smith. It can be found at www.thestrippodcast.com.

There are also two "alternative" weeklies in Las Vegas. That word is in quotes because the *Las Vegas CityLife* is owned by the *Review-Journal's* parent company and the *Las Vegas Weekly* is owned by the *Sun's* parent company, so neither function in the independent manner as alt-weeklies were born to do. Still, both take greater liberties with avant-garde writing and generally have more liberal slants than a family newspaper would, and *CityLife* carries a regular gay-issues column called "Slant" by longtime gay activist Lee Plotkin.

LEGAL ISSUES FOR GLBT TRAVELERS

Same-sex marriage is not recognized in Nevada, although several major resorts invite gay couples to wed in legally insignificant ceremonies in their chapels. State law prohibits discrimination against gays and lesbians in housing, employment, and public accommodations. Despite rumors to the contrary, prostitution is *not* legal in Las Vegas or anywhere in Clark County. It's only legal in Nevada counties with fewer than 400,000 residents, but local officials have also barred it in

the Carson City District and Lincoln County. There are no legal male brothels in Nevada, although former Hollywood Madam Heidi Fleiss has said she plans to open one in Nye County. However, Fleiss said her brothel would only cater to heterosexual women clients, not gay men.

LODGING

At first blush and based solely on its resort offerings, Las Vegas wouldn't seem like a gay-friendly environment. There's just one 47-room gay-owned hotel, no gay-owned casinos, and owing to county laws prohibiting guest homes, no legal gay (or straight) bed-and-breakfasts.

That said, this section proves that dozens of good options are available at a variety of price points where GLBT travelers will feel welcome and respected.

CODE:

A = art gallery

B = employees have same-sex domestic-partner benefits

C = convention space

G = on-site golf

M = movie theaters

P = gay porn in rooms

S = spa

W= permits same-sex weddings

77777= very expensive

7777 = expensive

777 = moderate

77 = bargain

7 = very cheap

A. THE SEVEN BEST PLACES FOR GAYS TO STAY

Bellagio

3600 Las Vegas Blvd. S.

Las Vegas, NV 89109

Reservations: 888/987-6667; www.bellagio.com; 77777

A, B, C, P, S, W

Grade: A+

Since Bellagio's debut in 1998, the Venetian, Mandalay Bay, and now Wynn Las Vegas have all opened. And still, this masterpiece of a Vegas resort-casino stands as the undisputed pinnacle of elegance and the center of gravity of the Strip. Simply put, nothing else compares to this Italian village-themed resort with its lengthy list of clever innovations and treats, from the signature dancing fountains and the $8 million blown-glass Dale Chihuly chandelier in the lobby to the Conservatory's stunning seasonal display of thousands of live plants tended to by more than 100 horticulturists. Plus, this is the only hotel in America with two AAA Five Diamond-rated restaurants, Picasso and Le Cirque. Yet beyond all that—beyond the high-end shopping, the Cirque du Soleil show, the Gallery of Fine Art, and one of the largest spas on the Strip—is the simple fact that service at Bellagio has the

attentive personal feel of a boutique hotel, even though it has a whopping 3,933 rooms.

Caesars Palace Hotel & Casino

3570 Las Vegas Blvd. S.

Las Vegas, NV 89109

Reservations: 800/634-6661; www.caesarspalace.com; 7777

B, C, P, S, W

Grade: A+

Two words: Celine Dion. Two more: Elton John. And did I mention by 2008, Bette Midler, too? The 40-year-old Caesars Palace, one of the original megaresorts, has enjoyed a rebirth in the past decade as a young, hip, fun hotspot at the center of the Strip where the shows, the shopping, and the scene is as gay-positive as anywhere. The rooms in the main tower could use some sprucing up—they're floral-print-bedspread plain, no different than a Holiday Inn—but since rooms are often incidental to what goes on elsewhere in a Vegas resort, they're adequate and offer some fantastic views of the Bellagio fountains. Pure, the nightclub owned in part by Ms. Dion, is among the most comfort-

able clubs for gays to be out and affectionate in. Plus, the newest tower, the Augustus, kicks it up a notch, with white down comforters, padded-leather headboards, and bathrooms with 17-inch flat-screen TVs.

Mandalay Bay

3950 Las Vegas Blvd. S.

Las Vegas, NV 89119

Reservations; 877/632-7800;

www.mandalaybay.com; 7777

B, C, P, S, W

Grade: A

Often, this bottom-Strip resort is referred to as the Mandalay *Gay*, because it seems to be disproportionately staffed by queers and it tends to attract loads of gay tourists. In addition, Mandalay Bay is one of the most complete resorts on the Strip, with a fleet of outstanding restaurants led by Aureole and Mix, excellent entertainment in *Mamma Mia!* and concerts at the House of Blues, as well as easy proximity to Luxor's frequent headliner concerts. Moreover, Mandalay's wonderful pool region—it spans 11 acres and includes a sandy beach with a wave pool, a topless pool, and a lazy river—comes with loads of notoriously hot lifeguards in cute red shorts. Some of the basic rooms in the main tower are strangely decorated—one had red vertical stripes for wallpaper and made it feel like you were sleeping inside somebody's pajamas—but THEhotel suites are spacious and post-modern comfy with their gray and black color schemes. The one lackluster side of Mandalay is the unimpressive shopping devoid of any significant name stores.

MGM Grand Hotel-Casino

3799 Las Vegas Blvd. S.

Las Vegas, NV 89109

Reservations: 702/891-1111; www.mgmgrand.com; 777

B, C, P, W.

Grade: A

When it opened, this place had a lot wrong with it, starting with an utterly tacky tribute to the *Wizard of Oz* that can still be seen to some extent in the rainbow-patterned carpets. Today, though, despite doing away with Judy Garland, Friends of Dorothy are exceptionally welcome here, right down to the marketing of its two-hour couples spa treatment to gays and offering a hair salon by that flamer Cristophe. They've also upgraded the restaurants in a big way, most recently by grabbing Joël Robuchon for his first U.S. eateries. If you can splurge big time, the Skylofts, 51 bi-level ultra-modern suites that start at $850 a night (see sidebar page 25), are the best and most stylish of the high-end room inventory in Las Vegas. And for a value option, try the modernist West Wing rooms, less expensive and not much wider than the plush king bed they contain, but appointed in a handsome gray-and-taupe scheme.

Palms Casino Las Vegas

4321 W. Flamingo Rd.

Las Vegas, NV 89103

Reservations: 866/942-7770; www.palms.com; 777

C, M, P, S

Grade: A

George Maloof's brilliantly hip hotel-casino gets it right where the Hard Rock fails, earnestly welcoming both gays and straights to the property with equal effusiveness. Maloof clearly understands that a party's not a party without a few queers around. The approach here is devoid of any judgments whatsoever, especially in the Fantasy Tower, where suites have "show showers" for strippers to get wet and entertain spectators in the living room. This unique property is a magnet for the Hollywood set, thanks to the Playboy Club and casino, the Rain in the Desert nightclub, and the hot steakhouse N9NE; it's also where Rosie O'Donnell and other gay stars participate on Bravo's diverse *Celebrity Poker Showdown*. Plus, Maloof regularly breaks open the bank to host major gay fundraisers for the community, including AFAN's annual Black and White Party and the 2006 National Lesbian and Gay Journalists Association awards soiree. (Full disclosure, my partner and I wed here in March 2007; see pages 22-23.)

Paris Las Vegas

3655 Las Vegas Blvd. S.

Las Vegas, 89109

Reservations: 1-877-796-2096; www.parislasvegas.com; 777

B, C, P, S, W

Grade: A

In 2006, Harrah's suddenly realized that this hotel could have great appeal to GLBT travelers and placed it at the forefront of its gay-media marketing efforts. Well, duh. With a pleasant gay-Paree sensibility—three feet of the half-sized Eiffel Tower actually jut into the casino—and an unbeatable center-Strip location that provides perfect views of the Bellagio fountains across the street, Paris is one of the more underrated hotels in town. One reason could be that Paris has failed to host anything but abysmal shows, though the latest try with

The Producers at least has a pedigree and an enormous gay following. The rooms could use some updating, but you get what you pay for and you tend to pay a lot less than you would at Bellagio and Caesars on the same corner. Mostly, though, this is the one property that has stridently pleaded for GLBT attention in a revolutionary way and, thus, deserves respect and loyalty. Even if you don't stay, stop in to gamble, see the show, or just kick back at Mon Ami Gabi, a Parisian street-side café where guests can watch humanity go by over a croissant—exactly as they would in the hotel's namesake city.

Wynn Las Vegas

3131 Las Vegas Blvd. S.
Las Vegas, NV 89109
Reservations: 888/320-WYNN; www.wynnlasvegas.com; 77777
B, C, G, S, W
Grade: A

Queer is stamped on pretty much every corner of Steve Wynn's newest $2.7 billion property. Every inch of the place was designed by flamboyantly gay designer Roger Thomas (see Q&A, page 28), who went to town with bursts of flowers, colorful tile mosaics, and dozens of gyrating parasols hanging from the ceiling in the main level. He even designed the sunken dining room at Alex as homage to *Hello, Dolly!* The show *Le Rêve* has very homo-suggestive action and the shopping is highlighted by a store from gay *Sex and the City* shoe outfitter Manolo Blahnik. The rooms, too, are sumptuous and clever, especially the innovation of mounting the flat-screen TV on a swivel on the wall so no armoire is required; the TV

MY BIG FAT GAY VEGAS WEDDING

On March 18, 2007, surrounded by family and close friends, my partner Miles Smith and I got hitched. No, it wasn't legal. No, not everyone in our families was thrilled with the whole thing, although those who attended were clearly in our camp and that's all that matters to us. And yes, it was the happiest day of our lives.

This being my own gay Vegas guide-book, it seemed appropriate to describe what we did and why. We didn't ship off to Massachusetts or some other jurisdiction where gay marriage or civil unions are available. Since we don't live there, doing so wouldn't give us any new rights here in Nevada and we are not, I'm fond of saying, "marriage tourists." You know, the gays who go wherever it's legal just because they can. Not us.

Odd as it may sound, this was my second gay wedding. My first took place in 1999 in Sedona, Arizona, to my first-ever partner, whom I met when I was 20 and ended up splitting from when I was 30. The first time out it was an over-the-top affair of nearly 100 people, a DJ, a fancy sit-down dinner, and a large wedding party. I went through it with conflicted feelings, since I knew there were problems in the relationship, and I later came to view the event as a debacle that heightened the humiliation and embarrassment of my break-up.

Two years after I became single for the first time in my adult life, I met Miles. I'd been recruiting members for the Vegas chapter of the National Lesbian and Gay Journalists Association; he's a TV producer. We'd emailed a bit before meeting on Oct. 1, 2004, at the Firefly, a Spanish tapas restaurant on Paradise Road. The attraction on many levels was instantaneous and we began building a life together. It wasn't but a week before we were using the term "boyfriend" to describe each other.

I was hesitant to have another wedding, but Miles and I were so much in love and I didn't have any of those doubts and fears I had on the first go-round. So I proposed to him on bended knee beside a roaring fire in a suite at a resort on Mount Hood, Oregon, in April 2006. He said yes.

We briefly considered holding the wedding in a chapel at one of the hotels.

MY BIG FAT GAY VEGAS WEDDING

Mandalay Bay, in particular, was our top choice. But then we discovered what a mill the Vegas wedding thing is—you get about 45 minutes to do your thing before they move you along to haul in the next group of people for their life-changing event. It seemed impersonal, rushed, and expensive.

Ultimately, we opted to rent a SkyVilla at the Palms, one of those 6,000-square-foot suites with the small private pools hanging off the building atop the new Fantasy Tower. This turned out to be a brilliant idea; even if you can't afford the $25,000 for that space, you could try a SkyLoft at MGM Grand or a penthouse suite at Bellagio, both for about $800. Point is, plenty of dramatic spaces are perfect for a cozy, intimate, non-cliché Vegas wedding. Best of all, you can stay as long as you like.

We hired the in-house caterers, who whipped up a turkey carving station, a mushroom-ravioli pasta bar, and a killer dessert tray. Which was lucky, because the cake we ordered from a cute French bakery on the west side was miserable and drippy, perhaps the only real disappointment.

We skipped the dancing and relied on our iPod to provide music. Our friend Mark created a slideshow of pictures of us that played on flat-screen TVs throughout the evening. And we had poker chips made up with our names and dates on them for guests to take. Mostly, though, we allowed the space itself to be the star, along with the two of us, and everyone seemed to know they were doing something different and special.

Most of all, we loved every minute. The ceremony, presided over by a liberal rabbi we found after being rejected by three others, was perfect. The rabbi, in fact, had never done a same-sex wedding and cried as he explained his own spiritual journey to a place where he was OK with this. You know you've done well when the clergy weeps at your nuptials, huh?

And now we move on to the next phase: adoption. Clark County happens to be very progressive about helping gays adopt foster children, so we hope within a year to be dads.

People—even gay people—wonder why we bothered to have a legally meaningless wedding at all. We look at it as the foundation of our life together and, even more important, the foundation of our child's family. She'll look at those pictures one day and she'll see us young, happy, in love.

Yes, such things exist here in the heart of Sin City.

can be seen from the couch or the bed by positioning it right. Plus, this is the only property on the Strip with an attached on-site golf course, designed by Wynn and Tom Fazio.

B. THE STRIP & VICINITY
I. EXPENSIVE

Four Seasons Las Vegas

Atop the Mandalay Bay Hotel-Casino

3960 Las Vegas Blvd. S.

Las Vegas, NV 89109

Reservations: 800/819-5053; www.fourseasons.com; 77777

B, C, S, W

Grade: A-

As with Four Seasons the world over, this one is the last word in personal service—right down to the pool attendants who spritz mist on your face when the heat is too intense. But this Four Seasons has something that none other does: easy access to a fantastic Las Vegas casino-resort, Mandalay Bay. The four floors of the Four Seasons rooms sit atop Mandalay's main tower. So just as the quietude and stuffiness of the Four Seasons is about to get to you, slip through what seems like a magic door near the ground-floor elevator and suddenly you're in the middle of a casino with great restaurants and shows. As a Four Seasons guest, you also have access to Mandalay's expansive pool area, or you can relax away from that ruckus at your own pool. The only downside is that the rooms are the same footprint as Mandalay's, so there's nothing especially spectacular about their layout or amenities beyond different duvets and overstuffed chairs. This Four Seasons also has the outstanding Charlie Palmer Steak restaurant and serves up afternoon tea at the Verandah lounge.

MONEY TO BURN

What's great about Vegas is that with unlimited resources comes unlimited luxury. Here are a few sure shots to impress your beau or trick.

- **Skylofts at MGM Grand:** Adorned like urban apartments, each two-level Skyloft includes at least five flat-screen TVs, a convertible shower–steam room, and so much Bang and Olufsen technowizardry that an attendant has to explain how it all works. Return from dinner to find the "champagne bubbles" massage tub already filled and a menu left by the "dream butler" asking which of nine pillow styles of you desire. (Starts at $690. 877/646-5638. www.skyloftsmgmgrand. com)

- **Bellagio Penthouse Suite:** Enjoy up to 2,000 square feet, with windows from which to peer down on the sensational dancing fountains. Plus, there's a wet bar, an expansive living room, and a his-and-hers bathroom. If you're thinking you won't need the "hers," it's worth noting there's a bidet in there. (Starts at $600; 888/987-6667; www.bellagio. com)

- **Skyvillas at the Palms:** A whole gaggle of you and your friends will dig taking up residence in one of the six suites in the new Fantasy Tower that have vagina-shaped swimming pools cantilevering off the edge of the building. Those pools are the perfect spot for some serious lovemaking, giving a sense of exhibitionism even though nobody can really see and a sense of adventure from the rush of being outside with sensational views of the Strip. Inside, the 6,100-square-foot one-story model has two bedrooms and five bathrooms that include showers with jets coming from every conceivable angle. (Starts at $25,000. www.palms. com. 866/725-6773.)

Hard Rock Hotel & Casino

4455 Paradise Rd.

Las Vegas, NV 89109

Reservations: 800/473-7625; www.hardrockhotel.com; 7777

C, P, S

Grade: B

The good news is: This is the only major casino-resort that's walking distance to the Fruit Loop cluster of gay bars and businesses. The bad news is: The first Vegas hotel to cater directly to the 20- and 30-somethings is unabashedly geared toward straight boys and their posses. It's not so much that there's anything homophobic going on here, it's just a popular and beautifully designed playground for heterosexual men. From the hard rock-n-roll theme with the Joint concert venue to the advertisements accentuating scantily clad women, it's clear who HR is trying to impress. In fact, many people complain about shoddy service, due to the fact that they're not (a) pretty enough and (b) straight enough. That said, the Hard Rock is known for attracting hot guys and music celebs, which can be fun to watch at the beach-themed pool, as long as you don't feel moved to ask any of them out. Rooms are plush, with feather pillows, expansive bathrooms, and 27-inch TVs; some have French doors instead of windows—and they open, too. (That's a novelty in the sea of hermetically sealed chambers that are standard at liability-conscious Vegas properties.)

Mirage Hotel & Casino

3400 Las Vegas Blvd. S.

Las Vegas, NV 89109

B, C, P, S, W

Reservations: 800/374-9000; www.mirage.com; 777

Grade: B+

The hotel-casino that kicked off the megaresort era in 1989 is noticeably less gay since Siegfried and Roy's act ended following a 2003 on-stage tiger attack. That said, the Mirage has held up remarkably well over its 18 years as its visionary, Steve Wynn, has moved on to build Bellagio and now Wynn Las Vegas. Everything that was to come—the free on-street entertainment, big spectacle shows, enormous hotel towers, an otherworldly environment—started here. The views from the rooms are somehow only enhanced by all that came after on the block, namely its neighbors Treasure Island, the Venetian, and the Caesars Palace expansions. True, the spa and rooms haven't been renovated in years, but it remains impressive to walk through the tropical domed walkway into the lobby past all those fresh orchids and bromeliads to see the sensational 20,000-gallon aquarium full of sharks and puffer fish behind the front desk. A new Beatles-scored Cirque du Soleil, *LOVE*, opened in 2006, and a planned overhaul of the property's signature exploding volcano attraction promises to provide this venerable favorite another infusion of freshness.

Venetian Resort & Casino

3355 Las Vegas Blvd. S.

Las Vegas, NV 89109

Reservations: 877/857-1861; www.venetian.com; 77777

A, C, S

Grade: B

This property could easily earn an A, except that this is a gay guidebook and the Venetian, owned by strident Republican conservative Sheldon Adelson, distinguishes itself with a sad trifecta: No same-sex weddings allowed, no gay porn offered, and no domestic-partner benefits provided to gay employees. Too bad, since the Venetian rivals Bellagio and the Wynn in scope, class, and comfort. The Venetian is essentially the

Q & A with Designer Roger Thomas

It should come as little surprise that some of the most fabulous and famous megaresorts in Las Vegas were the design brainchilds of a gay man. Roger Thomas, Steve Wynn's personal interior decorator, is responsible for the Mirage, Treasure Island, Bellagio, and Wynn Las Vegas. In that role, he's splashed up the toniest settings in Sin City with vibrant colors and real exotic plants. Thomas is the scion of a prominent Mormon clan in Las Vegas—his family name graces the Thomas & Mack Arena at UNLV—who met Wynn's wife when the two were on the board of the local dance company in the 1970s. Twice divorced from women, he wed his male partner of six years at the Wynn in April 2005, a week before the resort opened.

Q: What's different about designing a casino than another structure?

A: You have to be aware of who your clients are, about certain superstitions your clientele might have. You have to learn about other cultures so people from those cultures can feel lucky there. For instance, we don't use what used to be one of my signature things, white flowers. White flowers denote funerary arrangements to Asian cultures. Designing a casino is trying to make the casino a very important part, but not what the hotel is about. The hotel should still be about graciousness, drama, mystery, and romance.

Q: How did your prominent Mormon family respond to your being gay?

A: I was in my fourth decade when I came out and had been through two marriages. Everybody pretty much knew. When I called my sister, who was the first one I told, she said, "You know, Roger, nobody's going to be surprised. Is that OK?" They wanted to know how they could support me. I have two brothers who either are or were Mormon bishops and I've only experienced complete acceptance and support from them.

Q: You're a flamboyant dresser. Lots of polka dots and stripes. Did you always dress like that?

A: Always. I was always in costume. I've had my own personal style and that style has always been a bit in your face and somewhat dramatic. I'm the guy who showed up at black-tie functions in a heliotrope dinner coat. When I go to buy clothes, it's a very emotional experience. I choose what moves me.

Q: Does that flamboyance and queerness play itself out in your design?

A: I don't think it comes from queerness, no. I don't think all flamboyant people are gay. I've always had a love of color over non-color. I've always liked things that were slightly off.

Q: How does Las Vegas stack up in terms of culture?

A: It's one of the capitals of the world now. It's not the capital of ballet or opera, but there are more theater seats sold in Las Vegas than there are in New York City.

Q: Compare your two most important works, Bellagio and Wynn.

A: Bellagio was designed on the basis of classic Palladian and Tuscan architecture and detailing. The same precepts informed the design of the Wynn, but I also wanted to create a new language. Some people prefer Bellagio and some prefer Wynn. That's as it should be. I feel Wynn shows growth beyond Bellagio. With Wynn, we designed the entire experience from the inside out, which is the opposite of how we designed Bellagio.

Q: How has Steve Wynn reacted to your sexual orientation?

A: Steve's never questioned it; he's always accepted it. And we joke about it all the time. I'll tell Steve, "Well, I know you feel that way because you're straight. You can't help it. You were born that way and nobody's perfect."

Pond-side cabana seating at Bartalotta di Mare at Wynn is one of Roger Thomas' celebrated designs for the resort.

world's largest business hotel masquerading as a Vegas resort and is about to get even bigger in 2007 with the opening of the attached sister resort, the Palazzo. That is, there's enough pizzazz here with the Italian frescos, gondoliers along the Grand Canal, and the 60,000-square-foot Canyon Ranch Spaclub to forget that the place is attached to the biggest privately owned convention center in North America. The rooms are spacious, but misnamed; the "suites" are really not suites, but one large room in which the lounging and sleeping areas are separated by ... a step. Still, gay travelers will adore the Grand Canal Shoppes and the Guggenheim Hermitage Museum (which showed a daring Mapplethorpe exhibit late in 2006), plus *Phantom: The Las Vegas Spectacular* appeals to the show-tunes queen within us all. The Venezia Tower takes the rooms to yet another level, offering 9½-foot ceilings and 130-square-foot bathrooms. One more downside, though: A peculiar and oppressive floral perfume overwhelms the casino and lobby air like a bad deodorant.

II. MODERATE

Bally's Las Vegas

3645 Las Vegas Blvd. S.
Las Vegas, NV 89109
Reservations: 888/742-9248; www.ballyslasvegas.com; 7777
B, C, P, S, W
Grade: D

If ever a Vegas resort could actually bore someone, it's this one. Other than the campy *Jubilee!*, nothing of great interest beckons you to Bally's. It's just a huge hotel with a killer location that gets high room rates for the aforementioned reasons, but its most significant charm may be that it's attached, via a cobblestone walkway, to Paris Las Vegas. Bally's buffet is a notorious sickening disaster, there's nothing interesting about the shopping, and whereas other properties have a half-dozen room styles to choose from, Bally's has but two—a 450-square-foot room that the Web site disingenuously claims to be "among the most spacious" in Vegas and "a one-bedroom grand suite" that has, uh, a queen-sized Murphy bed in the sitting area.

Flamingo Las Vegas

3555 Las Vegas Blvd. S.

Las Vegas, NV 89109

Reservations: 888/308-8899; www.flamingolasvegas.com; 777

B, C, P, S, W

Grade: B+

Sometimes referred to by gays as the Flaming-O, here's all you need to know: The hotel with the pink neon marquee boasts gay flamingos and a sexually ambiguous penguin. Yes, seriously. But even be-

yond that, this place has come a long long way since Bugsy Siegel built and bankrupted it. It's not a perfect resort—the rooms are standard-issue fare with the exception of 500 they recently modernized—but it's an economical and convenient one at the center of the Strip with what's frequently cited as having one of the most expansive pool areas in town. The George Wallace show is a horrid mistake, but the Second City troupe is reliable entertainment and Toni Braxton began a long-term gig late in 2006. And the buffet has the advantage of overlooking the Wildlife Habitat, one of the few in town with a view of anything, much less exotic animals and fish.

GAY FLAMINGOS

Wildlife Habitat

At the Flamingo

Open: 24/7

Price: Free

Bubblegum hearts Pink Floyd. Really. And they're both boys. The couple, Chilean pink flamingos on display at the Wildlife Habitat behind the Flamingo Hotel-Casino, can be spotted by looking for the pair that hang out together and have bands on their right legs signifying they're male. Gosh, John Waters would be proud. The gender and sexual orientation of an African penguin named Turnip, however, are unclear. Its sex has never been ascertained, because taking blood for a test proved impossible, but "he" is believed to be male. Better yet, Turnip was purchased to mate with Olivia, the resort's only white-beaked penguin, but has shown no interest in females. Go see for yourself. The Wildlife Habitat— which also has black swans, helmuted guinea fowl, and ducks that apparently show no sign of queerness—is free and open 24 hours a day, although both the habitat and wildlife are hard to see after dark. Take in the penguin feedings and a brief lecture daily at 8:30 a.m. and 3:30 p.m.

Harrah's Las Vegas

3475 Las Vegas Blvd. S.

Las Vegas, NV 89109

Reservations: 702-369-5000; www.harrahslasvegas.com; 777

B, C, S

Grade: D

The flagship property of the world's largest gaming company began its life as a Holiday Inn—and it shows. There's nothing to the architecture. The rooms not only lack any charm, they haven't been upgraded in any significant way, possibly in decades. Harrah's is, however, in the thick of everything on the Strip and has a few amenities that make a nondescript hotel shine just a bit, namely the Olympic-sized pool, Rita Rudner's brilliant show, and the Ghirardelli ice cream shop in the Carnaval Court out front. Otherwise, there's little of interest here, gay or straight, and the rooms are frequently as expensive as such superior and similarly situated properties as Paris, Monte Carlo, and New York-New York.

JW Marriott Las Vegas Resort, Spa & Golf

221 N. Rampart Blvd.

Las Vegas, NV 89145

Reservations: 877/869-7777; www.marriott.com; 777

B, C, G, S

Grade: B

About 15 miles northwest of the Strip, this ambitious 459-room Palm Springs-style resort set on 50 acres embodies an entirely different realm. It's just on the edge of where the city ends, so it's a quick jaunt over to the exquisite Red Rock Canyon area, a favorite among locals for hiking, biking, and scenic driving. The rooms have small decks that peer out over the golf courses and the beautiful Spring Mountain range looming to the west. Plus, there's a 50,000-square-foot casino on the property and a free shuttle to the Strip that leaves eight times a day. Bottom line, however, is you'll find little of gay interest here and may be beset with an abiding sense that, by staying away from the action, you're missing something over there.

Las Vegas Hilton

3000 Paradise Rd.

Las Vegas, NV 89109

Reservations: 888/732-7117; www.lvhilton.com; 777

C, P, S

Grade: B

Think of this place as Caesars-lite, but in a good way. The two are comparably rich in old Vegas history—there's a statue near the casino of Elvis, who opened the property in 1969—and both are try-

STAR TREK: THE EXPERIENCE

Star Trek: The Experience

At the Las Vegas Hilton

888/GO-BOLDLY

Open: 11:30 a.m.–8 p.m.

Price: Tickets $35.99-$38.99

For whatever reason—perhaps it's the nonjudgmental world it presents—"Star Trek" has always been wildly popular among queer geeks. But even if you sensibly think "Star Trek" is tacky sci-fi camp, it's still no excuse for skipping this pair of simulated motion rides. The basic premise for both is the same: You end up on a vessel that's being attacked and your ultimate safety depends on some death-defying twists and turns. The newer ride, Borg Invasion 4D, which opened in 2003, has a ton of technological bells and whistles—it's filmed and projected digitally, the 3D glasses actually do *not* make you dizzy, your seats make you feel like you're moving, and you even get splashed with water. But the brute force of being all shook up by the old-fashioned original, which was originally called "Star Trek: The Experience" but was renamed when Borg arrived as "Klingon Encounter," is just as fun. (Full disclosure: The author of this guidebook once briefly dated a Borg.)

ing to modernize. Caesars has Celine, the Hilton has Manilow. Elton John fills in for Celine; Reba McEntire was filling in for Manilow for a while. See the pattern? Similar, but a stratum or two below. And while Caesars has upgraded its room stock with the Augustus Tower and added acres of shopping, the Hilton has done little with the drab rooms and offers no important shopping. Still, the property does have some fun features—the Star Trek Experience is a huge gay favorite—and its convenient monorail stop puts the property, a mile east of Las Vegas Boulevard, virtually on the Strip.

Luxor Las Vegas Resort & Casino
3900 Las Vegas Blvd. S.

Las Vegas, NV 89119

Reservations: 888/777-0188; www.luxor.com; 777

B, C, M, P, S, W

Grade: B-

That iconic pyramid with the phallic beam of light pointing skyward briefly got a whole lot gayer as home to Broadway's *Hairspray*,

but that failed and the showroom is now being primed for a Cirque du Soleil magic show. As a resort, Luxor has plenty of problems: The inside of the place is a confusing maze, none of the restaurants are notable, and the rectangular tower was built next to the pyramid by someone who didn't care that it would ruin the vista of one of the few architectural innovations in this city. If you stay, insist on a room in the pyramid itself, where you ascend on "inclinators" and the rooms have a fun angular and Egyptian aesthetic. One queer-related intriguing tidbit: The Luxor spa has always been notoriously cruisy.

New York-New York Hotel & Casino

3790 Las Vegas Blvd. S.

Las Vegas, NV 89109

Reservations: 888/696-9887; www.nynyhotelcasino.com; 777

B, C, P, S, W

Grade: B+

In recent years, New York-New York's efforts to be as edgy and urban as its namesake have included a strident marketing campaign aimed at the GLBT market, starting with the 2002 debut of risqué cabaret *Zumanity* from Cirque du Soleil. The rooms are strangely angular and have a Manhattan aesthetic that could have been cheesy, but somehow comes off as a charming homage. It's odd, though, that some of the windows overlooking the Strip are blocked by bulky homely armoires. Those seeking an adults-only getaway ought to be forewarned that the ersatz Coney Island arcade and the Manhattan Express roller coaster guarantee scads of young kids flying all over the place at all hours. Also, the pool is located directly below the crescendo for the roller coaster, meaning you get to hear the screams of riders every couple of minutes as you try to relax.

Monte Carlo Hotel & Casino

3770 Las Vegas Blvd. S.

Las Vegas, NV 89109

Reservations: 888/529-4828; www.montecarlo.com; 777

B, C, P, S, W

Grade: B

This sadly overlooked—even by its owners—and stately property just sort of blends into the landscape between New York-New York and Bellagio. It's as if they built the place and then decided to let it fend for itself, with only one attraction, the Lance Burton magic show, worth advertising. Neither the restaurants nor the shopping are worth a visit and the rooms are simple and functional. Indeed, the quilted white-checkered bedspreads are just as milque toast as the rest of the property. Still, it's a great location, it's clean, and the service is notably attentive. Best of all, room rates are frequently lower than its neighbors.

Planet Hollywood

3667 Las Vegas Blvd. S.

Las Vegas, NV 89109

Reservations: 877/333-9474; www.planethollywoodresort.com; 777

C, P, S, W

Grade: B+

The transformation from the second Aladdin to the Planet Hollywood Resort and Casino is still underway as this book goes to press, but an April preview in advance of the September 2007 grand opening shows that the ambitious plans of quirky Planet Hollywood CEO Robert Earl are sure to vastly improve it. They're totally overhauling the circuitous mess that was the front entrance and they've rid the place of almost all the trappings of Arabia, a loser of a theme in this post-9/11 world if ever there was one. Plus, they're adding a load of new restaurants, including the Earl of Sandwich (opened by an eighth-generation descendant of the guy who invented the sandwich!) and Alfredos, from the Italian family that invented Alfredo sauce. Still, the presence of the gay hotspot Krāve here doesn't make it a mecca for gay travelers, largely because—get this!—there's no way to get in without actually leaving the hotel and entering from an outside door. That, however, can't be laid at Earl or Planet Hollywood's feet, and the redesign of the rooms is particularly interesting, because they've promised that each of the 3,000 or so rooms will have authentic memorabilia from a different movie. Happily, when Earl took over, he also took over the wedding chapel, which had been subleased, and now they do same-sex weddings, too. That's a smart move, given the presence of Krāve and the Miracle Mile (formerly Desert Passage) Mall, two huge queer draws.

Rio All-Suites Hotel and Casino

3700 W. Flamingo Rd.

Las Vegas, NV 89103

Reservations: 800/752-9746; www.riohotelcasino.com; 777

B, C, S, W

Grade: A

Gay travelers would be forgiven if they took one look at this rainbow-drenched resort with occasional beefy male dancers shaking it in the casino as "Bevertainers" and thought this was, in fact, the elusive casino-for-queers that some folks have always hoped would arrive in Vegas. The Rio is not gay, per se, but it sure is happy—and happy to have all sorts of visitors, so long as they're seeking a good time. As themed hotel-casinos go, the Rio hits something of a perfect alchemy, with a festive party atmosphere featuring the noisy but fun Masquerade Show in the Sky show that floats above the casino floor seven times a day and spacious rooms with floor-to-ceiling windows. The hotel also makes good use of its height with the tower-topping sultry Voodoo Lounge bar and nightclub, which set the tone for the ultralounge trend that followed. The Rio is also known for its outstanding Carnival World and Village Seafood buffets, local favorites. And while the Chippendales stripper show is really for women, the ubiquitous billboards advertising it around the property are nice to look at. The only downside is that the Rio has no shopping of note and is off-Strip, but regular free shuttles run to sister properties Caesars Palace and Harrah's.

Treasure Island

3300 Las Vegas Blvd. S.

Las Vegas, NV 89109

Reservations: 800/288-7206; www.treasureisland.com; 77

B, C, P, S, W

Grade: B+

In recent years, the Treasure Island—known as the bastard child of Steve Wynn's creations on a block that also boasts Bellagio, Mirage, and the Wynn—has tried hard to make itself relevant to the hip crowd. Much of it has worked. While the renaming of the property as the "TI" didn't quite cut it (not even execs from parent company MGM Mirage actually call it that), the introduction of the Tangerine nightclub, Social House restaurant-club, and the elegant Buffet at Treasure Island have actually brought a newfound interest in this "older" megaresort. (It opened in 1993, which makes it like 65 in Vegas years.) Plus, Treasure Island still has *Mystère*, the first and best Cirque du Soleil show, but the rooms are dull—and those bedspreads are so loud as to be deafening. The hotel-casino also matured the pool area by taking out the slides that attracted lots of screaming young ones and doing away with the faux pirate-ship-deck motif. At the same time, the revamp of the free show out front on the pirate lagoon is kind of a disappointment for gay travelers, as they've replaced a lot of the sexy shirtless pirates with buxom scantily clad

"sirens." Neither show made much sense, so the loss of that eye candy was a bummer.

Westin Casuarina Hotel and Spa

160 E. Flamingo Rd.

Las Vegas, NV 89109

Reservations: 702/836-5900; www.westinlv.com; 777

B, C, P

Grade: B

The Westin is one of the few Vegas casinos catering primarily to business travelers—after a few attempts at a show, they decided to turn the showroom into a meeting venue—but that often makes it a great deal for leisure travelers. It's an excellent value, given the location a block east of the Strip, and it carries on the solid Westin tradition of simple tasteful elegance with those aptly named Heavenly Beds and Baths that everyone raves about. Plus, the Silver Peak Grill is one of the best coffee shops in town.

III. VALUE

Alexis Park Resort

375 E. Harmon Rd.

Las Vegas, NV 89109

Reservations: 800/582-2228; www.alexispark.com; 77

C, S

Grade: B+

The nicest non-gaming resort in Las Vegas, the Alexis Park is laid out with a Palm Springs sensibility: several small buildings scattered around a series of palm-tree-surrounded pools and Jacuzzis. It's an easy walk from here to the Fruit Loop cluster of gay bars and businesses, too. The staff and ownership are extremely gay friendly; this was the site of Vegas' first major gay convention when the National Lesbian and Gay Journalists Association came to town in 1998. At that time, the Strip hotels took little interest in hosting it. The Alexis Park's lack of a casino does tend to draw conventioneers, as well as families with small kids, but it's across the street from the Hard Rock if you need to cut loose. The property is, however, a couple miles east of the Strip, too far for most to walk, especially in the scorching Vegas heat. Worse, there's no shuttle for guests and the in-house restaurant is lackluster. Larger groups might like the bi-level Regal Suite, 1,275-square-foot digs with two bedrooms and a gas fireplace, to share expenses.

Bill's Gamblin' Hall & Saloon

3595 Las Vegas Blvd. S.

Las Vegas, NV 89109

Reservations: 888/227-2279; www.billslasvegas.com; 777

P

Grade: F

Run, don't walk, from this creepy tacky slum that survives solely because of its unbelievable location at the same corner as Bellagio, Caesars Palace, and Bally's. The air is viscous with smoke, the carpet is soiled, the rooms are small and seedy, the marquee entertainer is a 400-pound Elvis impersonator. Bill's (formerly the Barbary Coast) also has the reputation of being the Strip's worse "sweat shop," gambler parlance for the sort of place where the bosses watch you carefully and sometimes throw you out if you start winning. Worst place to work. The place does get raves for its nightclub, Drai's, but for the same money, you can dance at Pure. There aren't even any amenities—no pool, no spa, no wedding chapel, nada. This redneck hole is no place for a nice gay guy or gal to settle into, and the sooner they implode the place, the better. Ew.

Excalibur

3850 Las Vegas Blvd. S.

Las Vegas, NV 89119

Reservations: 800/591-6423; www.excalibur.com; 77

B, C, P, S, W

Grade: D

The largest and most unfortunate remnant of the early 1990s effort to court families, Excalibur is abjectly tacky—and not in a campy sort of way. It's a dorky King Arthur fantasy come to frightening life, with rooms notable for their low ceilings and less charm than a Days Inn. Plus, there are absolutely no interesting restaurants other than a steakhouse that earns some raves. The *Thunder From Down Under* ads with the bare-chested cast are cute, even if the show's a bore, and

if you're really that desperate for some beefcake, the *King Arthur's Tournament* show has some, too. But the only reason to stay here is that it's got a great location and the rooms are cheap. They're not *dirt* cheap, though, so again, the appeal is limited.

Orleans Hotel & Casino

4500 W. Tropicana Ave.

Las Vegas, NV 89103

Reservations: 800/675-3267; www.orleanscasino.com; 77

C, M, P, S

Grade: B+

The Orleans is popular among gays for a few key reasons: It's inexpensive, it's known for good service, its 24-hour Courtyard Café coffee shop is staffed with loads of gay-friendly waitresses with terrific senses of humor, and it's walking distance to queer Vegas' most popular Sunday evening watering hole, Charlie's. This off-Strip property is middle-brow and proud of it. Free regular shuttles run to and from the Strip.

Riviera Hotel & Casino

2901 Las Vegas Blvd. S.

Las Vegas, NV 89109

Reservations: 800/634-6753; www.rivierahotel.com; 77

C, S, W

Grade: B

The Riv is a classic Vegas joint in both the good and bad sense. Good in that it's got a very sexy vibe with a lineup of shows like *Crazy Girls* and *An Evening at La Cage* that scream out camp, fun, and a pro-gay attitude. Bad in that it's mildly seedy and run down—the place is 52 years old, after all—and harkens back to a less upscale time for Vegas. That said, you get what you pay for and in that sense, the Riv is a very good deal. Rooms are actually nicer than the smoky deliberately confusing casino would have you think, basic but clean. While the shopping and dining are lackluster, its location just north of Wynn and a little ways up the Strip from the Fashion Show Mall tends to make up for it. Plus, liberal groups and the porn industry frequently use the Riv's space for conventions.

Silverton Hotel and Casino

3333 Blue Diamond Rd.

Las Vegas, NV 89139

Reservations: 866/946-4373; www.silvertoncasino.com; 77

C, P

Grade: A-

As value options go, this is the little resort that could. It would seem to be the last place to find anything of interest to gays, but for a time there was even a daily show involving hot mermen in a 117,000-gallon saltwater aquarium. A new attraction is being developed, but until then the Silverton is still an excellent value about five miles south of the Strip. It opened as a low-brow destination, but has blossomed into a respectable venue that attracts some solid B-list entertainment—Paula Abdul and Hootie and the Blowfish have exclusive deals here—and offers surprisingly comfortable rooms for the price. The Sundance Grill, the hotel's 24-hour café, has a menu almost as expansive as any Cheesecake Factory—and the new muted brown and tan earth-tone scheme makes the place lovely. The hunting-lodge theme still persists, though, and one of the biggest attractions here is a giant Bass Pro Shop Outdoor World. Free shuttles take guests to and from the Strip regularly.

South Point

9777 Las Vegas Blvd. S.

Las Vegas, NV 89123

Reservations: 866/796-7111; www.southpointcasino.com; 77

C, M, P, S

Grade: B

Here's the bad news: This new yellow-everywhere resort gives visitors a sense that they're trapped in a vat of whipped butter. From the casino to the rooms, everything is strangely jaundiced. The good news is, if you get over that, you'll probably be pleased with this simple property that doesn't aspire to be anything more than a less expensive but respectable choice about three miles south of the Strip. The rooms are basic, but have some lovely views of the mountains, as well as 42-inch plasma flat-screen TVs. And the South Point also provides free regular shuttle service to Mandalay Bay. Not a bad deal for the money. Plus, they've got a sand volleyball court and an equestrian center for horse shows and events, which is a little different for Vegas.

Stratosphere Hotel-Casino

2000 Las Vegas Blvd. S.

Las Vegas, NV 89104

Reservations: 800/998-6937; www.stratospherehotel.com; 7

C, S, W

Grade: B-

Gay travelers seems to love this big, tall, uh, tower. It is, after all, among the best deals on the Strip—$35 room specials are common—and without a doubt one of the most distinctive features on the Vegas skyline. The tower is a Vegas gimmick that takes full advantage of its gimmickry, what with the city's death-defyingly best thrill rides plopped atop the tallest free-standing building west of the Mississippi River (1,149 feet) and an observation deck that gives you a 360-degree view of the Las Vegas Valley. Still, there's a reason this place is so cheap; it's in a pretty rough area known locally as the Naked City and there's no longer a free shuttle south to the prettier parts of the Strip. Now that Mandalay Bay opened Mix atop THEhotel, which you can ascend for free before 10 p.m. for a better view, there's less reason for people not staying at the Stratosphere to brave the area. But the rooms are nice enough, the buffet is surprisingly decent, and the Sahara monorail station is less than a mile's walk south.

LAS VEGAS STRIP

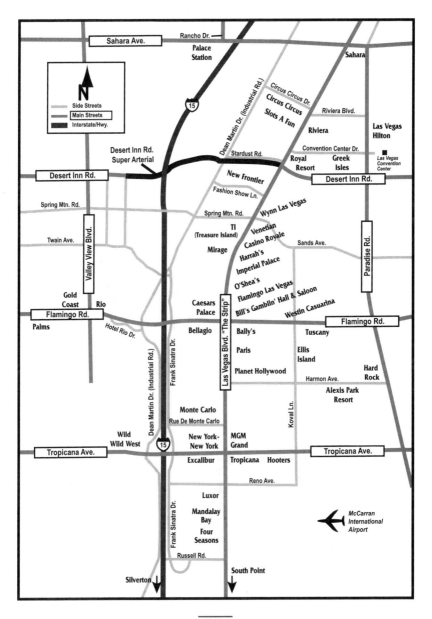

DOWNTOWN LAS VEGAS

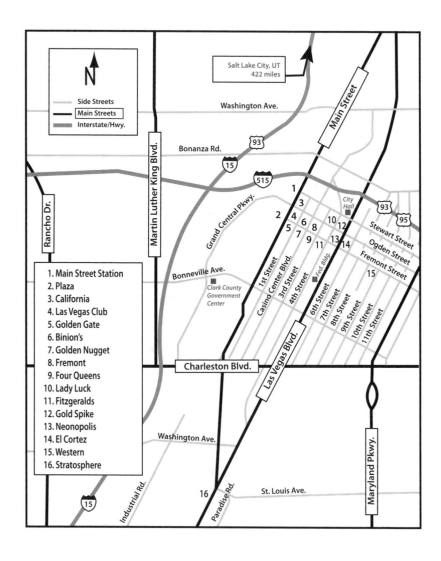

N

Side Streets
Main Streets
Interstate/Hwy.

Salt Lake City, UT
422 miles

Washington Ave.

Main Street

Bonanza Rd.

93

15

515

Rancho Dr.

Martin Luther King Blvd.

Grand Central Pkwy.

City Hall

93

95

Stewart Street

Ogden Street

Fremont Street

Bonneville Ave.

Clark County Government Center

1st Street

Casino Center Blvd.

3rd Street

4th Street

Fed Bldg

6th Street

7th Street

8th Street

9th Street

10th Street

11th Street

Las Vegas Blvd.

Charleston Blvd.

Maryland Pkwy.

Washington Ave.

Industrial Rd.

15

Paradise Rd.

St. Louis Ave.

16

1. Main Street Station
2. Plaza
3. California
4. Las Vegas Club
5. Golden Gate
6. Binion's
7. Golden Nugget
8. Fremont
9. Four Queens
10. Lady Luck
11. Fitzgeralds
12. Gold Spike
13. Neonopolis
14. El Cortez
15. Western
16. Stratosphere

BOULDER STRIP

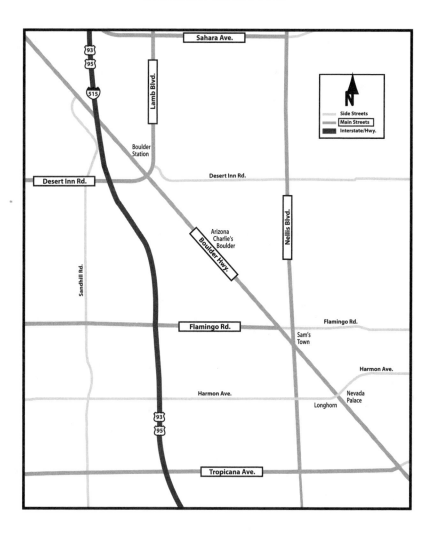

TWO WORTHY FRUIT LOOP OPTIONS

The themed and gussied-up Las Vegas hotels and resorts require careful deconstruction, but two reasonable and respectable chain choices in the Fruit Loop bar cluster area are affordable and convenient to both the Strip and to Vegas' gay nightlife.

Ⓐ Amerisuites (4520 Paradise Rd., Las Vegas, 89109; 877/774-6467): The closest lodging to the gay bars, this is a plain standard hotel. It's right next to the funky Hofbräuhaus German Restaurant and Beer Garden, a fun place to eat one meal and probably spot Siegfried and Roy, who frequent the place. Amerisuites also provides guests a free breakfast buffet. www.amerisuites.com.

Ⓑ Embassy Suites (4315 Swenson St., Las Vegas, NV 89119; 702/795-2800): Owned by Hilton, this all-suite property offers clean comfortable rooms with wireless Internet, free made-to-order breakfast, and a cute indoor pool. www.embassysuites.com.

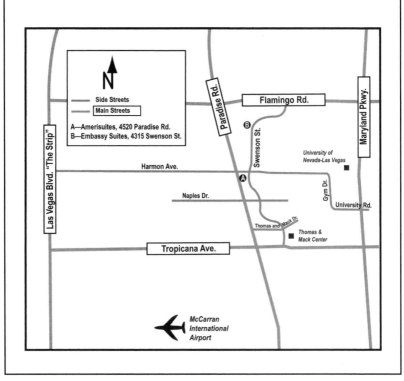

AWAY FROM THE STRIP

Four Queens Hotel & Casino

202 Fremont St.

Las Vegas, NV 89101

Reservations: 800/634-6045; www.fourqueens.com; 7

Grade: D

This entry acts almost as a disclaimer: There's nothing queer about the Four Queens except, umm, its name. It's not a homophobic property by any stretch, but it's a rundown dump typical of most of the downtown Las Vegas properties from the El Cortez to Fitzgeralds that aren't written up in this book because their names don't evoke a drag show. The place has no pool, spa, or even cable TV. The one saving grace, aside from the dirt-cheap postage-stamp-sized rooms and 25-cent-minimum crap tables, is Hugo's Cellar, a beautiful old-Vegas gourmet room where every woman gets a rose. And, boys, we're sure you can have one, too, if you ask.

Golden Nugget

129 Fremont St.

Las Vegas, NV 89101

Reservations: 800/846-5336; www.goldennugget.com; 77

C, P, S

Grade: B

The downtown Las Vegas core of casinos is largely a wasteland of small low-brow properties left over from the earliest days of the city, which started here on Fremont Street. The only hotel-casino in the sector that comes close to rivaling the Strip in respectability is the Golden Nugget, with its clean rooms and a boisterous casino. Recent turnover in restaurants and entertain-ment does make its amenities a bit more of a gamble, but the Golden Nugget offers the sort of attentive service you expect on the Strip at a significantly lower price.

Green Valley Ranch

2197 Paseo Verde Pkwy.

Henderson, NV 89012

Reservations: 866/782-9387; www.greenvalleyranchresort.com; 7777

C, M, S

Grade: A-

This sensational 201-room boutique resort is, along with its new sister property Red Rock Resort, the only major off-Strip offering that doesn't leave you feeling like you're missing out on anything by being a few miles away from the action. Most of the best elements—a happening casino, a celeb-studded nightclub, a gorgeous spa—are all here. Among its many triumphs is its expansive outdoor pool-cum-nightclub, the eight-acre Whiskey Beach. There's a sand beach, vineyards, even an amphitheater for concerts. In addition, Green Valley Ranch is adjacent to the hot new high-end shopping center called The District, where 45 stores from Anthropologie and William-Sonoma are laid out in a Main Street-style. The hotel also provides a free shuttle to and from the Strip.

Red Rock Casino Resort Spa

11011 Charleston Blvd.

Reservations: 866/767-7773; www.redrocklasvegas.com; 777

C, M, S

Grade: A

The first billion-dollar Las Vegas resort off the Strip is so spectacular that it makes it difficult to believe this is from the same folks who brought us Palace Station. The Fertitta family and Station Casinos have come a long way, spending their bucks lavishly, but also wisely, to take full advantage of Red Rock's location in the far northwest corner of the city just beneath the Spring Mountain range. The color scheme of earthen rouge tones fits perfectly, but this hotel isn't just a superficial triumph; there's functional thought put into how people will use the space. To wit, the lobby is physically pretty, with its dramatic 60-foot crystal chandelier, and convenient in that it's steps from the guest elevators, but it also has a large bar area with plush couches and chairs, which gives you a comfy place to wait for friends, something few Vegas resorts have. The rooms are far nicer than most standard rooms on the Strip, what with all that marble and hardwood as well as VoIP phones, plasma TVs, and an iPod docking station. The property's central focus is the three-acre Sandbar Pool Backyard, a pool and beach with a fountain and blackjack tables that also is a killer setting for concerts. If there's one thing keeping Red Rock from total greatness, it's that the food falls flat, particularly at the oppressively noisy T-Bones steakhouse. And, of course, there's the handicap of being 11 miles from the Strip. Red Rock admirably attempts to overcome this problem with a spacious casino and hip Cherry nightclub and, yes, being away from the rest is sort of the point. Nonetheless, many baffled guests will be left thinking, "What's something this nice doing all the way out here?"

Ritz Carlton, Lake Las Vegas Hotel

1610 Lake Las Vegas Pkwy.

Henderson, NV 89011

Reservations: 702/567-4700; www.ritzcarlton.com; 777

C, G, M, S, W

Grade: D+

Why anybody would come to Las Vegas and stay 17 miles southwest of Las Vegas Boulevard in this boring little joint is beyond us. Gay travelers in particular will feel a sense of being marooned on the edge of town with old straight couples who couldn't bear the noise and action on the Strip. This Ritz is a badly designed Mediterranean-style resort on the shores of the man-made Lake Las Vegas with boring shopping, a low-energy casino, and not a single dining option to get excited about. The rooms, too, are dull, and the walls are so frighteningly thin that you can hear the neighbor's alarm clock—or whatever else there is to hear over there. On the nominal plus side, the hotel is just up the street from Hoover Dam and has free shuttles to the Strip. As wedding settings go, this may be the most un-Vegas option for those who don't want to marry in a casino, since the chapel is separate.

BLUE MOON RESORT

Blue Moon Resort

2651 Westwood Dr.

Las Vegas, NV 89109

Reservations: 866/798-9194; www.bluemoonlv.com; 77

Grade: B+ (A- if you're really horny)

Las Vegas' first—and to date still the only—gay resort is a difficult one to diagnose. On the one hand, there's a charm and comfort to being in an all-queer, virtually all-male, clothing-optional environment. And while it's tucked away in a strange industrial complex away from the center of Vegas action, it's just two miles from the Commercial Center cluster of gay bars and businesses and it's not that much farther, really, from the Strip than the Palms or the Rio. The property itself was renovated from a Travelodge into something somewhat nicer; the 47 rooms might be considered Travelodge-luxe, some with leather furnishings and modernist décor. But it's the pool that most folks come for, having been upgraded to feature a Jacuzzi grotto and a 10-foot waterfall. Recognizing its isolated location, a café sells coffee, Danish, salads, and sandwiches, and on Sunday afternoons from April to October a free poolside barbecue is held. And this year, they've added free continental breakfast to guests.

The problem is that the place sits very precariously on the border between sexy and sleazy and the steam room can occasionally function as a de facto bathhouse, thanks to a rather inexpensive $15 day pass for locals or non-guests. Not, as Seinfeld might say, there's anything wrong with that, but all visitors—in-

cluding those gay travelers *not* looking for a hypersexualized atmosphere—ought to be fairly warned.

Pricewise, though, it can be a terrific bargain, with room rates peaking at a very rare $179, and more often down around $119 per night.

Q & A with Gay Dealer Christopher Allegra

For the past decade, Christopher Allegra has worked as a dealer at the MGM Grand.

Q: What's the secret to winning?

A: You know, people ask me that all the time. I meet guys online and when they hear [I'm a dealer], they ask me. There isn't any answer. It's all about money management and luck. There's nothing I can do as a dealer to help them out.

Any good tips on how to get comps?

A: Pretty much anybody can get comped for the buffet at the MGM Grand if they're playing for a while and they have a players card. To get anything more significant, you have to bet, say, $25 a hand for so many hours. You have to be the one to ask, though. Unless you're a real high roller, they won't come looking for you to offer you comps.

Is the casino a homophobic place?

A: Not really. I don't discuss my personal life with the guests, so I haven't been the target of anything. And gamblers usually don't insult one another at the high-limit tables where I work.

At the MGM Grand, you cater to the super-rich. How are they treated differently?

A: In a place like the MGM Grand, the rules are shaded in

gray, because we deal with the wealthiest people in the world. You tend to do things you wouldn't ordinarily do, like allowing them to touch the cards. Some have special requests, like that only men can be in the room or only women, or maybe that there need to be nine glasses of water on the table and nobody is allowed to touch them. If they suddenly want a Nathan's hot dog and there's no Nathan's hot dog around, I'm sure they'll get it. But it's rewarding. The biggest tip I ever got from a single customer was $260,000. He was someone very famous in business, but we're not allowed to say who. All our tips are put in a pool and shared evenly with all the dealers working that shift, so I didn't get all that money, but it was definitely a good day.

But you can talk a little about the celebrities you deal to, right?

A: Oh, sure. I see them all. Matt Damon, Ben Affleck, Charles Barkley, Bruce Willis, and Demi Moore. Bruce Willis can be great when he's there to have a good old time, and other times he's not so happy. Our job is to be flexible like that. We have to know when to joke and when to just shut up. I know there are all the gay rumors about Ben and Matt, but they're really just close friends. JLo was here when she was with Ben and regardless of what you've heard about her, from what I've seen she's really sweet.

Any big goof-ups?

A: Not by me, but you always have to be careful. These people bring their wives or girlfriends or boyfriends or husbands or whatever and you never know who's who exactly. Another dealer I know says to one guy, "Oh, where's your wife?" and she's sitting right there, but last time the guy had come in with someone that's not his wife. Discretion is important.

FO4OD

If there's a section of this book that's almost impossible to define in gay terms or from a queer perspective, this is it. A show or a resort can be analyzed for sensuality or camp, but how is a humble filet mignon or a fancy piece of salmon supposed to prove itself worthy? In the absence in Las Vegas of both a large number of gay-owned restaurants and any known instances of routine overt homophobia in dining, divining a method of determining what to recommend—and what to recommend avoiding—is probably a gay guidebook writer's greatest challenge.

Yet the new Vegas is a culinary destination and gay people are notorious foodies. Thus, what you'll find is a careful concoction of a fellow gay foodie's intensely subjective views baked together with the gay-friendly reputations of chefs and restaurateurs. Wonderful and lousy restaurants alike are identified as such, regardless of whether they host gay fundraisers and the like, but those that are socially conscious receive the notation "GF" for "gay friendly" or "GO" for gay-owned.

Do not misread. Those without such designations aren't necessarily known as anti-gay, but there's been no word that they've made any pro-gay efforts.

Dig in!

A. STRIP-AREA RECOMMENDATIONS

LEGEND:

GF = gay-friendly

GO = gay-owned

Price ranges:

$ = under $15 per person

$$ = $15-$29 per person

$$$ = $30-$49 per person

$$$$= $50-$99 per person

$$$$$ = $100+ per person

1. AMERICAN-CALIFORNIAN

(GF) Charlie Palmer's Aureole (at Mandalay Bay, 702/632-7401; prix fixe $69, tasting menu $95): Sure, that four-story wine tower at the center of the restaurant with the black-clad "wine angels" ascending on winch-and-pulleys to fetch ordered bottles is a gimmick, but gosh, what a gimmick! Aside from its modernist chic, the wine tower is the harbinger for what can only be described as an oenophile's wet dream: a 50,000-bottle wine list to complement Charlie Palmer's exquisite food. What's more, the restaurant is the first anywhere to offer the eWinebook, a tablet PC on which diners can search the wine list by price, region, varietal, or pairing with dishes. You can also watch the wine

angels do their deed from streaming video taken live inside the tower. *Absolutely fabulous*: Herb-crusted Pacific halibut with potato/snap pea pancake in wine sauce.

(GF) Mix (at Mandalay Bay, 702/632-7777; $$): This brilliant and gorgeous restaurant-cum-bar on the top floor of THEhotel at Mandalay is an Alain Ducasse stroke of genius. It's actually difficult to decide where to sit: outside staring down the city's best bird's-eye view of the Strip, or inside enveloped by a chandelier made up of 15,000 pieces of blown glass. The food's amazing, too, an appropriate, uh, mix of Ducasse's varied interests, from American and other staples. *Absolutely fabulous*: The salmon with the spicy shallot marmalade.

The Palm (at the Forum Shops, 702/732-7256; $$): This sleek intimate restaurant gives the feel of slipping into a calm shelter for an excellent lunch-time salad or dinner filet. Also, it has a surprisingly respectable wine list for such a low-key joint.

Nob Hill (at MGM Grand, 702/891-7337; $$$$): Quiet, slow-paced, and luxurious, plus fantastically creative American cuisine and doting service—it's all you might hope for. Michael Mina transports the best of his Bay Area classic to the Strip. *Absolutely fabulous*: the signature lobster pot pie.

(GF) Spago (at the Forum Shops, 702/369-0360; $$$): Homage must be paid to the man who started Vegas' celeb-chef craze, Wolfgang Puck. When it opened in 1992, Spago was the first high-end restaurant here and many pundits declared it doomed. Confused diners, in fact, thought the open counter by the kitchen was some sort of buffet line and queued up. It's an oldie, then, but a goodie, starting with addictive cheese-baked flatbread and working through the California-cuisine menu. Plus, it's a great way to rest from all that intense buying in Caesars' Forum Shops. *Absolutely fabulous*: the marinated pork with Gruyère spaetzle.

Terrace Pointe Café (at Wynn Las Vegas, 702-770-7100; $$): Light and airy, this café shows the depth of care the overall Wynn operation invests in food, by providing top-notch meals even at the glorified coffee shop. In particular, the chopped Cobb is probably the best you'll find in Vegas. Plus, the lines move very quickly.

(GF) Wolfgang Puck Bar and Grill (at MGM Grand, 702/891-3000; $$): The trend today is to tuck restaurants away from the clamor of the slots, which is generally wise. Puck's recently renovated open-air eatery smack-dab at the crossroads of a major

ring-a-ding-ding casino is a welcome exception. Diners are sheltered enough by the partitions to hear their companions, but the jolt of energy from the surroundings adds to the meal somehow. And this is Puck at his most engaging, fun, and—for Vegas—affordable.

2. ASIAN

(GF) Ah Sin! (at Paris Las Vegas, 702/967-7999; $$): That exclamation point in the name is well-earned. This affordable pan-Asian eatery with killer views of Bellagio's fountains across the street is a terrific surprise, with a variety that ranges from outstanding sushi to Peking-style stuffed chicken wings and terrific Chinese noodles. That said, the "sin" part is the decadent desserts befitting a place associated with Paris. *Absolutely fabulous*: Orange crème brulée.

(GF) Chinois (at Caesars Palace, 702/737-9700; $$$): Wolfgang Puck wouldn't seem like the fellow you'd trust with Asian food, but this fusion of Chinese and California cuisine yields spicy Shanghai lobster, so-called "firecracker" shrimp, and orange-soy-glazed roasted chicken. *Absolutely fabulous*: stir-fried Peking duck with red wine pineapple sauce.

Red 8 Asian Bistro (at Wynn Las Vegas, 702/770-3463; $$): One of Wynn Las Vegas' most affordable options is also one of its best, a rollicking off-the-casino-floor dining room where authentic Asian cuisine isn't watered down by Western expectations. The chef, Malaysian-born Hisham Johari, defected from Noodles at Bellagio, where he routinely made special-order dishes for Chinese travelers. *Absolutely fabulous*: scallion pancakes.

Sushi Roku (at Caesars Palace, 702/733-7373; $$): Yes, this is the fourth outlet in the U.S. for this franchise. And yes, you do feel a bit like there are some personal touches missing. But the sushi is always fresh and beautiful, which is really the heart of the matter. *Absolutely fabulous*: yellowtail sashimi.

Tao Asian Bistro (at the Venetian, 702/388-8338; $$$): Attached to one of the hippest new nightclubs in Vegas, Tao diners sit beneath a mammoth Buddha in a restaurant modeled after—then made far grander than—an uber-trendy Manhattan namesake. The menu offerings are surprisingly authentic—a dragon roll with eel and Kabayaki sauce, for instance—and decidedly skewed toward exotic seafood plates. Still, the Peking duck may be the best you'll find on the Strip.

Tsunami Asian Grill (at the Venetian, 702/414-1980; $$$): Tucked in the back of the Grand Canal Shoppes is a little-noticed bi-level restaurant that is a magnet for Asian conventioneers, which tells you something right there. The menu reflects a hard-core Asian aesthetic, with a huge section on sushi and plenty of Thai chicken and beef offerings. *Absolutely fabulous*: coconut salmon.

REJAVANATE

reJAVAnate

3300 E. Flamingo Rd.

Las Vegas, NV 89121

702/253-7721; www.rejavanatecoffee.com

Hours: Daily 6:30 a.m.–9 p.m.

The only gay-owned non-Starbucks coffeehouse in Vegas is also where most of this book was written. A star of *Phantom: The Las Vegas Spectacular* at the Venetian and a star of *Forever Plaid* at the Gold Coast opened this warm living-room-style lounge, where excellent lattés and sensational pastries are served by an adorable college-aged staff who play Scrabble during the slow periods, but snap to attention whenever necessary. The walls feature art by local painters and photographers, which is changed out monthly. Plus, free wi-fi! And to prove that you don't need Starbucks to concoct a convoluted drink, my personal favorite here is the non-fat, sugar-free, decaf vanilla-hazelnut Rechiller. Try it.

3. BURGERS AND SANDWICHES

Fatburger (various locations including on the Strip at 3763 Las Vegas Blvd. S., 702/736-4733; $): I know, I know. What self-respecting homo would eat at place with a name like that? Well, one looking for an amazingly thick burger at a reasonable price. The turkey burger's great, too. Yes, the place has a sock-hop-in-the-ghetto feel to it, but if you're not comfortable, then take it out and enjoy elsewhere.

In-N-Out (various locations including near the Strip at 4888 Dean Martin Dr., 800/786-1000; $): This cult-favorite West Coast chain serves up excellent burgers with a delicious relish and French fries from potatoes cut before your eyes. The menu seems simple, but there's a secret menu on their Web site, code words every clerk knows for a no-carb burger and extra-crispy fries.

'wichcraft (at MGM Grand, 702/891-1111; $): An excellent and quick offshoot of NYC's Craft and Vegas' Craftsteak, offering creative sandwiches, like grilled Gruyère and caramelized onions on rye, for $6-$9.

Capriotti's (various locations including near the Strip at 324 W. Sahara Ave., 702/474-0229; $): Slightly off the Strip, this no-frills sandwich shop offers the city's best hoagies, including the capastrami (pastrami with all sorts of condiments) and the Bobbie, a turkey-cranberry-stuffing mess.

4. CUBAN

Florida Café (inside the Howard Johnson's Hotel, 1401 Las Vegas Blvd. S., 702/385-3013; $): The neighborhood is seedy and the HoJo is rundown, but the god-honest truth is this food is as authentic Cuban as you'll find in Vegas. The local Cuban community reveres this place, so you know it's where you need to go when you're hankering for plantains and ropa vieja. Plus, it's reasonable.

5. FRENCH

(GF) Alex (at Wynn Las Vegas, 702/770-7000; $$$$$): A dining room this sumptuous can be risky. Once diners descend from the broad *Hello, Dolly*-inspired staircase to settle into a dining room of dramatic orange drapes and tall windows, will the food be as lovely? At Alessandro Stratta's masterful restaurant, the answer is yes. From the chilled quail terrine appetizer to the poached chicken in a black truffle sauce and a hearty pear napoleon

with mascarpone and sauternes, Stratta's superlative Franco-Italian cuisine would be worth eating on a park bench. *Absolutely fabulous*: the braised short rib of beef.

Eiffel Tower Restaurant (at Paris Las Vegas, 702/948-6937; $$$$): Let's see: You're at on the 11th floor of a replica of the most romantic structure on the planet, eating amazing gourmet food while peering out over the fountains in front of the Bellagio. Fantastique, non? Indeed, this could have been a tourist trap—see the Top of the World restaurant entry—but with a AAA Four-Diamond award, it's clearly earned its respect. *Absolutely fabulous*: cream of sweet garlic soup.

Le Cirque (at Bellagio, 702/693-8100; $$$$): One of the ultimate splash-outs in Vegas, Le Cirque is a pricey though worth-it version of the New York eatery that nurtured such latter-day Vegas star chefs as Daniel Boulud and Alessandro Stratta. This is one of the few places in town, though, where you will definitely feel out of place if you don't dress up. *Absolutely fabulous*: lobster salad with black-truffle dressing.

Lutece (at the Venetian, 702/414-2220; $$$$): Chef David Feau, a protégé of the legendary Guy Savoy, succeeds in replicating his New York success by taking Lutece's brilliantly executed French cuisine and adding Vegas panache—including tables overlooking the Venetian's Grand Canal. The foie gras with apple purée and balsamic reduction and the Muscovy duck with carrot purée are lovely. *Absolutely fabulous*: the Valrhona chocolate mousse cake with vanilla sauce.

(GF) Mon Ami Gabi (at Paris Las Vegas, 702/944-4224; $$): One of the best examples of a restaurant that fits a hotel's theme, this place offers tres-bien crepes and steak frites in a real Parisian atmosphere, complete with outdoor seating along the Strip on a first-come, first-serve basis. Perfect for brunch.

Picasso (at Bellagio, 702/693-7225; prix fixe menus are $90 or $100): Even if the menu had no masterworks, dining amid Picassos worth $30 million would be art enough. But thanks to James Beard winner Julian Serrano's roasted scallops and his lobster, scallop, and shrimp boudin, this Bellagio restaurant is not just a museum outing. Bored with Pablo's paintings? There's always the view of the dancing fountains outside. *Absolutely fabulous*: roast pigeon with risotto.

Restaurant Guy Savoy (at Caesars Palace, 702/731-7731; seven-course prix fixe menu is $300): Yet another elusive famed French chef has chosen Vegas for his American debut, this time in a space in the new Augustus Tower at Caesars that's all high ceilings and checkered hard-wood paneling and views of Bellagio's fountains. The 950-bottle champagne bar is an easy place to drop a few

hundred—or thousand—dollars just waiting for your table to get ready, but if you're here already, you probably can afford that, along with the food, which is delightfully classic French fare. Truffles are all over the menu—in the soups, the brioche, even the butter. *Absolutely fabulous*: chocolate ganache with tonka beans.

6. ITALIAN

Corsa Cuchina & Bar (at Wynn Las Vegas, 702/770-7000; $$$): This comfortable, relatively casual, but exceptional dining option at the otherwise pricey Wynn offers up a feast of classics with new twists, from veal lasagna to seared scallops in a fig-caper emulsion. A recent redesign vastly improved the setting, which was previously very dark, so that now light pours in from the sports book, the casino, and the hallway to the poker room. An odd bonus is that Corsa has the most comfortable chairs in Vegas dining. No, really. My partner asked where we could buy some. *Absolutely fabulous*: goat's-milk-ricotta-stuffed ravioli.

Fiamma Trattoria (at MGM Grand, 702/891-7600; $$$): The wavy beauty of the restaurant isn't the only success here. Every dish, it seems, offers some delicious twist, from the short-rib-stuffed ravioli to the semolina pasta with black truffles. This Fiamma is an excellent edition of a New York favorite. *Absolutely fabulous*: sage roasted organic chicken with white-truffle potatoes.

Il Fornaio (at New York-New York, 702/740-6403, and Green Valley Ranch Resort and Spa, 2300 Paseo Verde Pkwy., Henderson, 702/492-0054; $$): Outstanding affordable but tasty Italian in a city overwhelmed by overpriced pasta. The lasagna ferrarese is wonderful, as is the fresh bread for dipping in olive oil.

Nove Italiano (at the Palms, 702/942-6800; $$$$): By now it seems *de rigueur* that new hotel towers in Vegas be topped by an upscale restaurant that relies largely on its impressive vistas and modernist décor to impress customers. It's a welcome surprise, then, that the latest offering from the folks who brought us the stargazing-central N9NE Steakhouse would show a mastery of Italian that would make it a worthy recommendation even without the sensational sidelong views of the Strip from the 51st floor of the property's Fantasy Tower. In keeping with the hetero-sexy theme of the building, giant topiaries of the female form stand sentry by floor-to-ceiling windows in the outer dining room and wall-mounted 42-inch plasma screens rotate images of classic artwork. The signature dish is the monochromic Spaghetti Nove, loaded with lobster, shrimp, crab, scallops, and calamari and prepared at a cooking station at the restaurant's center by a chef who has no other job. And all that seafood's no aberration; the menu is loaded with such offerings as tuna tartar and Maine lobster in a cannoli shell and a striped bass unobtrusively dipped in a sun-dried tomato vinaigrette.

Rao's (at Caesars Palace, 702/731-7267; $$): A 110-year-old Spanish Harlem institution that's impossible to get into finally decides to branch out and end up as one of the few truly affordable upscale joints on the Strip? Well, sure, if you figure that the whole point of opening up other locations is to give more people the opportunity to indulge in those trademark meatballs in a uniquely tangy marinara, while protecting the Manhattan exclusivity of the quaint original. Yes, the Vegas offering loses the intimacy of the New York joint—there's a printed menu, the two replica dining rooms come off as a bit cheesy, and owner Frankie Pellegrino is unlikely to lead sing-alongs out west. But what does translate at this five-times-larger version is the freshness and authenticity of century-old recipes brought to life by Pellegrino's son and daughter-in-law, who use buffalo mozzarella so fresh it makes a diner pause to regard it, and serve a spinach-and-sage ravioli that may have improved on the New York version. Some dishes do suffer—the cheesecake isn't quite up to the greatness of its NYC counterpart—but the pollo scarpariello that features pieces of chicken bathed in white wine and arrayed with a mélange of colorful and spicy peppers packs a surefire wallop.

7. MEXICAN

(GO) Border Grill (at Mandalay Bay, 702/632-7403; $$$): Lesbian culinary icon Susan Feniger (see Q&A, page 86) and her business partner Mary Sue Millikin, known famously on Food Network as the "Too Hot Tamales," offer colorful interpretations of Mexican staples in an equally vivid cantina-style restaurant, with outdoor seating overlooking Mandalay's pool area.

Pink Taco (at Hard Rock, 702/693-5525; $$): With a name like that, you'd expect preening little queer Latino waiters, but no such luck that we could see. The décor is, however, festive—if a little noisy—and margaritas are generous. It's standard-issue Mexican, but tasty and good value.

8. OLD VEGAS

Bootlegger Bistro (7700 Las Vegas Blvd. S., 702/736-4939; $$): About a mile south of the bottom of the Strip is this gem, a 55-year-old bistro owned by the family of the former lieutenant governor, herself a former lounge act. It's open 24 hours, has excellent Italian eats and breakfast food, and B-listers like Clint Holmes and *Mamma Mia!* stars show up on Mondays after 10 p.m. for a very Old-Vegasy celebrity karaoke.

Center Stage (at the Plaza, downtown, 702/386-2110; $$): No promises on the quality of the food or service, but the Plaza is a likable dump and this restaurant provides that old-school feel. It also provides a killer view of Glitter Gulch.

Hugo's Cellar (at the Four Queens, downtown, 702/385-4011; $$$$): A thoroughly elegant paean to mid-century French chic, this place is so handsomely old-school that every lady gets a rose, and all dinners come with chocolate-covered fruit for dessert. Expensive, but worth it.

Luv-It Frozen Custard (505 E. Oakey, 702/384-6452; $): This classic walk-up dessert stand just off the main drag of Las Vegas Boulevard not far from the Stratosphere is a 30-year-old family-owned tradition for Vegas. The custard is always smooth and there are different flavors every day.

Peppermill Restaurant and Lounge (985 Las Vegas Blvd. S., 702/735-4177; $$): This thatched-roof greasy spoon has lost a bit of its onetime Rat Pack panache, but it's still a 24-hour non-casino diner with swooping rainbow-colored booths right on the Strip. Penn Jillette and a colleague hatched the idea for the horrible *The Aristocrats* film here, but don't hold that against it.

Piero's Italian Cuisine (355 Convention Center Dr., 702/369-2305; $$): An iconic haunt and one-time major mob hangout, as recently as 2005 the Feds were still busting Mafia suspects here. Oh, and the eats are solid Italian fare.

9. SEAFOOD

Bartolotta Ristorante di Mare (at Wynn Las Vegas, 702/770-3463; $$$$): Milwaukee chef Paul Bartolotta relocated here to open an Italian seafooder at the new Wynn Las Vegas. His reward—and ours—is this stunning "lakefront" eatery on the secluded side of a man-made mountain that shields guests from the ruckus on the Strip. The menu includes a flavorful baked pink snapper with oregano and artichokes, and five preparation choices for whole fish: roasted, grilled, or cooked in lemon, tomato, or wine sauce. Bartolotta was a finalist for best new restaurant in the 2006 James Beard competition. *Absolutely fabulous*: sheep's-milk ravioli.

(GF) Restaurant RM (at Mandalay Bay, 702/632-7777; $$$): Chef Rick Moonen closed up his successful and acclaimed New York joint to head to the desert, a gamble indeed in a town where most tourists

are programmed to want a good steak. The result is extraordinary, a restaurant that serves, by far, the best and freshest of the sea, flown in daily. *Absolutely fabulous*: any salmon dish.

10. SOUTHWEST

Bobby Flay's Mesa Grill (at Caesars Palace, 702/731-7731; $$$): Everyone who ever met Julia Child, it seems, is opening a place in Vegas—and not always with impressive results. But Food Network star Bobby Flay proves he has the substance to back up his TV style with Mesa Grill, a rare gourmet alternative to the French and Italian restaurants dominating the scene. The menu allows for real adventure in the form of smoked-chicken quesadillas topped with avocado and garlic crème fraiche. *Absolutely fabulous*: New Mexico spice-rubbed pork tenderloin with a bourbon-ancho chile sauce.

11. SPANISH

(GF) Firefly (3900 Paradise Rd., 702/369-3971; $): This is a rocking Spanish tapas hotspot just off the Strip, with dishes like bacon-wrapped dates and marinated lamb chops for $4-$10. Special note: This was the scene of my first date with my partner. A terrifically romantic sweet spot for Vegas.

(GF) Café Ba-Ba-Reeba (at Fashion Show Mall, 702/258-1211; $$): This reproduction of a great Chicago eatery is something the Strip could use more of: moderately priced and eclectic cuisine with outdoor seating. Dishes like cured pork loin with manchego cheese run $5-$10 each.

12. STEAKHOUSE

Craftsteak (at MGM Grand, 877/793-7111; $$$): James Beard Award winner and Top Chef star Tom Colicchio's Vegas edition of his NYC instant-classic Craft is nearly flawless—nearly, that is, because service can be slow. But the simplistic industrial décor—exposed light bulbs hanging from the ceiling, metal mesh for booth partitions—reflects a certain back-to-basic approach to a chophouse. No frills here—just straight-up fine steaks and fish. *Absolutely fabulous*: cinnamon monkey bread in dipping sauce for dessert.

N9NE Steakhouse (at the Palms, 702/933-9900; $$$): This is the celeb steakhouse of choice and for good reason. The 20-seat champagne-and-caviar bar is the perch from which to see and be seen. Fortunately, the food's as spectacular as the movie and recording stars who frequent the place. *Absolutely fabulous*: ground Kobe beef burger with applewood-smoked bacon, aged Vermont cheddar, and grilled onions.

StripSteak (at Mandalay Bay, 702-632-7414; $$): Watch out, Wolfgang Puck. San Francisco restaurateur Michael Mina is fast becoming the Vegas eatery mogul of choice, especially with his newest and perhaps most varied entry, StripSteak. The new Mandalay Bay steakhouse is Mina's fourth restaurant on the Strip, putting him second only to Puck, who has eight. Mina is known best for his seafood at Michael Mina Bellagio, Nob Hill, and Seablue, and here he moves on to several clever renditions (starting at $25 and escalating fast) of what the majority of Vegas visitors crave, a good piece of meat. From slow-poached prime rib to pork in a kumquat-jalapeno glaze, this is an example of pan-American cuisine done right. As is always the case in high-end Vegas, the design here is at least as important as the food, with the back wall made up of wood blocks stacked in a checkerboard style in an effort to transmit the message of modern, minimalist, and rustic all at once.

SW Steakhouse (at Wynn Las Vegas, 702/770-3463; $$$): It may get tiresome at Wynn to see the resort's namesake's name and initials everywhere, but at least as it pertains to this steakhouse, it's a synonym for incredible. From a table alongside the Lake of Dreams, try the chef's takes on lobster gazpacho and Alsatian spaetzle. Oh yeah, the steak's amazing, too. *Absolutely fabulous*: blueberry shortcake with mint ice cream.

B. OFF THE STRIP

Here's a menu of local favorites worth venturing away the Strip for.

(GF) Café Heidelberg (610 E. Sahara Ave., 702/731 5310; $$): When your hankering for a nice thick German sausage takes hold, head over to this delightful little spot. No *shadenfreude* here, just overwhelming portions of classic German dishes served by a harried German hausfrau of a waitress. The gay monthly, *QVegas*, had its offices a couple doors down until 2004, which should give you some idea how gay-friendly they are.

(GF) Harrie's Bagelmania (855 E. Twain Ave., 702/369-3322; $):
A brilliant and homey little bagel joint that's the closest thing to those East Coast Jewish breakfast houses—right down to a cranky and loving grandma-type waitress, Roz! A favorite of local gay couples and, of course, local Jewish families, although it's not kosher.

India Palace (505 E. Twain Ave., 702/796-4177; $$): A beautifully appointed Indian room with the city's best *na'an* and a sensational chicken *tikka masala*. Service is attentive, if a little icy. The lunch buffet is a good deal, too.

(GF) Lindo Michoacan (2655 E. Desert Inn, 702/735-6828; $$): Lindo is among the best Mexican restaurants not just in Vegas, but in the nation. The joint is so much more than the standard burritos and tamales. Javier Barajas learned this distinctive regional cuisine from his grandparents long before immigrating to the U.S., and the results are some tangy sauces and unusual combinations, plus lots of seafood. The bacon-wrapped shrimp, for instance, is a far cry from Taco Bell. Fair warning, though: The family has two other restaurants, Bonita Michoacan and Viva Michoacan, but they're nowhere near as good, for some unclear reason.

Joyful House Chinese Cuisine (4601 Spring Mountain Rd., 702/889-8881; $$): Las Vegas' Chinatown is, essentially, a series of themed shopping centers with lots of Asian stores. But the best Chinese in town is, fittingly, along that strip. Stick to the old standbys, sweet-and-sour chicken or broccoli beef, or be adventurous and try something exotic like shark-fin soup. Not cheap as Chinese goes, but worthy.

Lotus of Siam (in Commercial Center, 953 E. Sahara Ave., 702/735-3033; $$): Ask the top gourmet chefs in Vegas where they go for Thai and they'll send you to this unassuming storefront in the Commercial Center strip mall. Lucky for us queers,

Commercial Center is also a gay-bar cluster, so this makes for a perfect bite before hitting the Spotlight or the Apollo. That's some hot curry paste they use here, though, so calm your buds with the heavenly sticky rice with mango and coconut cream.

Metro Pizza (various locations, including inside the Ellis Island Casino, 4178 Koval Ln., 702/312-5888; $$): All you really need from a respectable pizza is a taut crust and tasty tomato sauce. The rest takes care of itself. Metro's got both down to a science, plus a cannoli to ruin your diet for.

(GF) Paymon's Mediterranean Café and Hookah Lounge (two locations, at 4147 S. Maryland Pkwy., 702/731-6030; 8380 W. Sahara Ave., 702/804-0293; $$): Paymon saved up as a dishwasher, then hit it

MONEY-TO-BURN SELECTION

Robuchon at the Mansion (at MGM Grand, 702/891-7358; prix fixe menus are $225 for 6 courses, $360 for 16 courses): Las Vegas took a seat at the most elite of culinary tables when it became the first North American city to lure French maestro Joël Robuchon. Robuchon at the Mansion is a timeless triumph, with a handsome main dining area lit softly by a mammoth tear-drop crystal chandelier that hangs from a 17-foot ceiling and a massive black fireplace that burns real wood. Diners choose from either a 10- or 16-course prix-fixe menu—both of which are among the world's most expensive such menus—that vary by season, but reliably carry such perfect openers as Oscetra-caviar-topped asparagus and entrées as pan-fried sea bass with lemongrass foam and stewed leeks. Absolutely fabulous: the expansive bread cart offering 10 varieties of rolls baked with flour imported from France, including one with ham baked into it.

big with a brilliant Middle Eastern restaurant that bustles from lunch hour to midnight, thanks to the Arabian silk-draped hookah lounge and the tangy spreads on the shwarma in a pita and the vegetarian platters. This perennial Best of Las Vegas winner is also a huge patron of the gay community, donating gift certificates for just about every fundraiser around.

Panevino Ristorante & Gourmet Deli (246 Via Antonio, 702/222-2400; $$): With its dazzling views of the Strip and the McCarran runway, this beautifully designed Italian spot turns out to boast pretty solid Italian cuisine, too. Try the ravioli di aragosta (ravioli stuffed with lobster, shrimp and leeks).

(GF) Strings (2222 E. Tropicana Ave., 702/739-6400; $): If ever there was a neighborhood restaurant for homos, it's this cute and incredibly inexpensive Italian restaurant about three miles east of the Strip. Such fancy dishes as pork tornadoes are delectable and cheap at an all-inclusive $12. What's more, this place crawls with queers, from the waitstaff to the clientele.

(GF) Tinoco's Bistro (1756 E. Charleston, 702/678-6811; $$): A big favorite among gay diners on their way to the First Friday arts crawl in downtown Vegas, Tinoco's is in a weird location (butting up against a muffler shop) and is a little cramped. But the food is lovely Italian fare made by Enrique Tinoco himself, who's been in Vegas forever. Very quaint and homey.

(GF) Trumpets Restaurant (2450 Hampton Rd., Henderson, 702/614-5858; $$$): Perched atop a hill about 10 miles south of the Strip is Trumpets, with its big picture windows showing off a unique and sensational view of the Strip. Groups of gay men who live in this area, known as Anthem, flock here for an expansive and pricey Sunday brunch. Also, dinners are spectacular, with a menu that includes an outstanding chateaubriand to chew on, along with an unsurpassed night view of the valley.

C. DON'T GO

Vegas-goers are offered loads of bad choices. It's probably as important to know what to miss as it is to know what to spend your money and time on. Opinions vary, but the following fail in my book—which this is!—so avoid.

Batista's Hole in the Wall: Wall-to-wall scarefest. Disgusting family-style food, inebriated frat boys with coupons everywhere, a totally obnoxious experience all around.

Bouchon (at the Venetian): Hopes were high for this bistro from Thomas Keller of French Laundry fame. But the food was average at best and the service was hands-down the worst we've ever endured. Sadly, that's actually what we expected from what others had said about it.

Bradley Ogden (at Caesars Palace): Ogden has a great reputation, and seeing him wander his restaurant floor regularly, he seems like an affable fellow. But his food has little imagination and you'll kinda wish he'd go back into the kitchen.

Burger Bar (at Mandalay Bay): Hubert Keller believes he's re-inventing the hamburger, but all he does is overload it with foreign objects that don't belong there. Plus, some of the wait staff are unnervingly creepy.

Carnegie Deli (at the Mirage): Lots of NYC imports hold their own here, but this one is as much a tourist trap as the original. Big fat sandwiches, sure. But for a prettier penny than is necessary. Insult to injury: The matzoh ball soup's a dud.

Diego (at MGM Grand): Perhaps the most expensive and boring Mexican food ever. There's nothing interesting here—not the menu, not the décor, not even a cute waiter.

Fin (at the Mirage): Our new favorite example of a gorgeous restaurant that doesn't live up to its décor. The dining room is beautiful, with purple bulbs of blown glass hanging dramatically from the high ceilings. Sadly, the food was costly and bland. Yawn.

Hard Rock Café (outside the Hard Rock Hotel): Remember when these places were the hippest restaurants on the planet? When you weren't anyone unless you wore one of their T-shirts? What was that, 1985? Move on, people.

Harley Davidson Café: Yes, there's a whole category of gays who love motorcycles, and not just the dykes-on-bikes variety. But this place is an obnoxious zoo, the closest thing you'll find on the Strip to redneck country. I'd worry for any homo's safety who tried to hold his boyfriend's hand here.

L'Atelier (at MGM Grand): How bizarre that this sister eatery to the amazing Joël Robuchon at the Mansion would be so miserable. The food is pedestrian. The requirement that parties of less than four sit at the noisy counter with little space is peculiar. And the décor evokes that of an upscale version of Chili's. Especially at these astronomical prices, one word comes to mind: Yikes.

Margaritaville (at Flamingo): What? Huh? Sorry, there's Jimmy Buffet music blaring from every friggin' direction and slobbery straight drunks everywhere. Also, my burger's overcooked and the fries are cold.

Okada (at Wynn Las Vegas): Here's a Japanese restaurant where the waitress warns you not to order the sushi, because it will take 45 minutes to prepare. Huh? A beautiful space, a wasted opportunity.

Red Square (at Mandalay Bay): A noisy crowded Russian mess. The food was decent, but for that kind of money—about $50 a person—you ought to be able to get out of your seat without slamming into a neighboring diner.

Rosewood Grille: A big billboard with the tuxedo-clad guy holding a lobster should be a good clue that this is a tourist trap. Trust me, there are classier places to go for a lobster, like Restaurant RM.

Shibuya (at MGM Grand): Do not be deceived by the décor, which is admittedly sensational. It will only disappoint you further when you get your undercooked fish and your spoiled sushi. Two of four of us up-chucked here. What a disappointment for one of the most eye-popping spaces in the entire restaurant universe.

Top of the World (at the Stratosphere): This one-time superb gourmet eatery now relies solely on its gimmick, sitting atop the Stratosphere and revolving. But Mix at Mandalay Bay now offers better food and a better view. Don't waste your time.

G. FIVE WORTHY BUFFETS

The old wisdom was that buffets were unhealthy, tacky, and cheap feeding frenzies for the great unwashed. But like everything else in Vegas, the buffet has been reinvented and upscaled. Many remain stuck in the past motif, but the following five are worthy of even discriminating palettes.

Carnival World

At the Rio

702/777-7777

Price: $15–$25, depending on meal

Hours: Mon.-Fri., 7 a.m.–10 p.m.; Sat.–Sun., 7:30 a.m.–10 p.m.

Known for its outstanding selection and fine quality, the Carnival World offers a decidedly Asian bent with a made-to-order noodle bar and loads of dim sum and sushi. When locals go looking for a megaresort buffet, here's where they head. Another plus: Automated payment kiosks help hasten the lines.

Cravings

At the Mirage

702/791-7223

Price: $15-$35 depending on meal

Hours: Mon.–Fri., 7 a.m.–10 p.m., Sat.–Sun., 8 a.m.–10 p.m.

This is a successful attempt at reinventing a buffet as an upscale restaurant, complete with a sleek design by Le Cirque architect Adam Tihany. Tihany created a large central dining area with

a high ceiling and terrazzo floors inlaid with onyx, surrounded by 13 cooking stations where highly regarded chefs prepare food in front of you. The Chinese selections in particular are spicy and authentic for those of us who have lived in China, and the macaroons on the dessert bar are addictive.

Buffet at Bellagio

At Bellagio

702/693-7223

Price: $15-$35

Hours: Breakfast Mon.–Fri. 8–10:30 a.m.; lunch Mon.–Fri. 11 a.m.–3:30 p.m.; dinner Mon.–Thurs. 4–10 p.m., Fri.–Sat. 4–11 p.m., Sun. 4:30–10 p.m.; brunch Sat.–Sun. 8 a.m.–4 p.m.

Yes, it's expensive. And yes, it's worth it. A buffet with Kobe beef, Mako shark, and smoked sturgeon? It could only be at Bellagio. And the décor, following the Tuscan theme with plush leather seats and cream-lime walls, makes you almost forget that it's a buffet at all. The make-your-own pasta bar is loaded with choices and the weekend-night meals typically feature lobster and steak. Plus, here's an insider tip: Walk right in, sit down at the bar at the back, and pay the bartender for the buffet. No waiting!

The Buffet at Wynn

At Wynn Las Vegas

702/770-3463

Price: $16-$36

Hours: Mon.–Fri., 8–10:30 a.m., 11 a.m.–3:30 p.m.; Sun.–Thurs., 4–10 p.m.; Sat.–Sun., 8 a.m.–3:30 p.m.; Fri.–Sat., 4:30–10:30 p.m.

Sticking with the hotel's effort to bring in as much natural light as possible really pays off in the buffet, turning the glass atrium dome entrance, decorated with fruity topiaries, into a light and airy comfort

zone. It also, some-
how, adds credibility
to the food, which
includes many buffet
staples, but also one
of the only made-to-
order salad bars in the
city. Dirty trick with
the desserts, though;
the "diet" ones are
"no-sugar-added," not

sugar-free, so they'll kill you.

Le Village Buffet

At Paris Las Vegas

702/946-7000

Price: $15-$25

Hours: Daily 7 a.m.–10 p.m.

Bon appetit, indeed! Here's the only hotel buffet that fits its prop-
erty-wide theme well and delivers absolutely sensational food. From
the look of the place, modeled after a French village, to the food stations representing various Gallic regions, this is the sort of transportive
experience we'd hope other hotels could try to employ. Oh, there's
plenty of non-French food, but why bother when homemade crèpes
and such a variety of cheeses await?

Q & A with Susan Feniger

Back in the mid-1990s when Las Vegas still suffered a reputation as a culinary wasteland, openly gay celeb-chef Susan Feniger and her business partner, Mary Sue Milliken, saw an opportunity. With their Food Network program "Too Hot Tamales" winding down and business at their Border Grill and La Ciudad restaurants in Los Angeles heating up, they decided to open a second Border Grill at a soon-to-open Las Vegas megaresort called Mandalay Bay. Feniger, 53, lives with her partner  of 11 years in L.A., but commutes every other week to Vegas to check on what has turned out to be the most successful of their properties.

Q: You saw the potential for Vegas as a food destination before many others. Why?

A: I thought it would be a great market for us. It felt like a growing market. We had a show on Food Network and expanding just made lots of sense. We got in early on. Not as early as Spago, but we were definitely in the first wave of a lot of name chefs.

Q: Surely you had culinary colleagues who questioned why you'd go there.

A: People were questioning Vegas, yes. People were saying it's very difficult to hire good employees, that we'd have to dumb down our concepts for the Vegas traveler.

Q: Have you?

A: No, not really. We put fun tacos on the menu. We do interesting ceviches. I mean, yeah, at lunchtime, we could be doing 800 to 900 patrons and we will sell a lot of quesadillas and tacos. But I can't say we don't do that in Santa Monica, too. It might be a little bit more extreme in Vegas, but I don't find that people in L.A. are ordering in a more sophisticated fashion. Maybe a little bit, but not dramatically.

Q: You're really the only celebrity chef who's openly gay. Why do you think that is?

A: Gosh, I've been out for so many years, I don't even think about it. But you know, for many years, I was the same way. I'd be out in terms of my own restaurants and everyone I dealt with and knew. But when it came to be interviewed by the *L.A. Times*, I wasn't hiding it, but I wasn't openly talking about it. And when we had a show on Food Network, I was less hesitant to be openly verbal about it. People fear it'll affect their business and their careers, that they won't get hired or get a TV show. But I don't even think about it anymore.

Q: Are you involved in the lesbian community in Las Vegas?

A: No. When I'm in Vegas, I just fly in, work all day and night, go to sleep, then go home. I don't go to clubs in L.A. or in Vegas. That's not something I do. The most involved I get, I guess, is that I'm very supportive of the gay center, of HRC, of Outfest. That's really how I'm most involved in the gay community, hosting fundraisers and that kind of thing.

SHWS

Girls! Girls! Girls! That's always been Vegas' entertainment calling card. But at long last, times really are changing. Now you can also see plenty of boys, gay-inclusive shows, major-league headliners, and Broadway imports. If you're not entertained here, it's your own fault.

Beefcake-O-Meter ( ): A rating of the aesthetic quality of the production regardless of its general artistic merits. Scale is 1-10.

Overall Quality: A grade on the artistic merits of the production irrespective of what sort of skin is offered. Gay-friendly and homophobic content is taken into account in formulating this grade.

A. THE FIVE BEST

Elton John: The Red Piano
At Caesars Palace
888/435-8665
Fri.–Sun., Tues.–Wed. at 7:30 p.m. when in town
Price: Starts at $100
BEEFCAKE-O-METER:
OVERALL QUALITY: A+

The minute the titillating video of Pamela Anderson pole-dancing to "The Bitch is Back" gives way to a mammoth inflatable banana and

suggestively placed cherries, you know Sir Elton has ushered in a new era for Las Vegas Strip entertainment. He and director Dave LaChappelle have taken Celine's theater and used that space in a way that Ms. Dion just isn't capable of, no matter how earnest. And he hardly even rises off his piano bench! The atmospherics are enough, along with John's classic music—he offers both salacious carnal imagery and some seriousness, as in the sad video for "Don't Let The Sun Go Down On Me." It's both old and new, thoughtful and funny, irreverent and genuine all in a 90-minute span. What's more, it's clear, in particular from the antics in "Pinball Wizard"—rich with Sin City video footage, imagery, and mockery—that in order to save the Vegas show form, Elton and producer David LaChappelle wanted to reinvent it.

KÀ

At MGM Grand

702/891-7777

Tues.-Sat. 6:30 and 9:30 p.m.

Price: Starts at $69

BEEFCAKE-O-METER: ♪ ♪ ♪ ♪ ♪ ♪

OVERALL QUALITY: A

Here's the one example in Las Vegas of technology and art coming together in a comfortable complementary way. The stage at Cirque du Soleil's fourth of five concurrent shows is the star, able to perform stunning feats of hydraulic magic, such as transforming from a three-dimensional boat to the side of a mountain before your eyes. Cirque uses it to change scenes in a way at least as amazing as the acrobatics that tell the story of twins being separated by evil forces. In the end, the only redeeming quality of the two bad guys is that they seem to have been some sort of couple. When one dies, the anguish is sort of touching.

Mamma Mia!
At Mandalay Bay
877/632-7400
Sun.–Thurs. 7:30 p.m., Sat. 6 and 10 p.m.
Price: Tickets start at $49.50
BEEFCAKE-O-METER: 💪 💪 💪 💪 💪 💪 💪 💪 💪
OVERALL QUALITY: A

What could be more queer than a ditzy musical scored to ABBA music in which a gaggle of well-toned shirtless studs actually undress the lead male character on stage and slip him into a skimpy spandex wetsuit while singing "Lay All Your Love On Me"? There's a story in

here somewhere—something about a young girl trying to figure out who her father is—but even in that effort a gay surprise awaits her. The only off-key note is when one of the female lead's friends, a likely candidate for lesbianism, instead ends up turning all girly-girl in swooning over the man's-man of male leads. Hurry and see it, though; the show's slated to close in summer of 2008 to make way for yet another Cirque production.

Mystère

At Treasure Island

702/894-7722

Wed.–Sat., 7 and 9:30 p.m., Sun. 4:30 and 7 p.m.

Price: Start at $60

BEEFCAKE-O-METER: ꒷ ꒷ ꒷ ꒷ ꒷ ꒷ ꒷ ꒷

OVERALL QUALITY: A+

Las Vegas' first—and to my mind still the best—permanent Cirque du Soleil show, this dream-like production offers eye-popping acrobatics, clever humor, and a catchy soaring score. And a bonus: a classic scene in which two shirtless Adon-

ises lift and twirl one another, at many points with their faces inches from each other's crotches. In the pre-*Zumanity* era, this was the hottest homoerotic moment in Vegas and, done with such class and taste, it remains immensely satisfying.

Phantom: The Las Vegas Spectacular

At the Venetian

866/641-7469 or phantomlasvegas.com

Sun., Mon., Wed., Fri., Sat., at 7:30 p.m., Tues. and Sat. at 10:30 p.m.

Price: Starts at $75

BEEFCAKE-O-METER:

OVERALL QUALITY: A+

You already know how this goes: Young Christine sings with melancholy about her lust for both a handsome aristocrat and an opera-house squatter. Oh, and a big light fixture will crash. Ah, but this is the Vegas version and, unlike every other Broadway attempt here, that means they throw in an over-the-top thrill-ride element that befits this razzle-dazzle town. The $40 million theater is designed to give you the feel of being inside that Parisian opera house and the special effects—including the one-ton chandelier that hurtles down and stops 10 feet over the audience—startle from beginning to end. Purists may moan about the shorter 95-minute running time, but Andrew Lloyd Webber himself chopped it down, so get over it. Two Phantoms, Christines, and Carlottas divide the work with five performances apiece in this edition, but everyone is remarkably excellent. It's worth noting, though, that one Phantom, Brent Barrett, is openly gay, a refreshing instance of a lead performer in a non-drag role in Vegas not being in the closet.

THE REST

A New Day ...
At Caesars Palace
702/474-4000
Thurs.–Sun., 8:30 p.m.
Price: Start at $87.50
BEEFCAKE-O-METER: 🍖 🍖 🍖 🍖 🍖 🍖 🍖 🍖 🍖
OVERALL QUALITY: B+

The oddest thing happened in the nearly five years since Celine Dion became the queen of Las Vegas: This show grew on me. Big time. I was always a huge fan of Celine's music and she fronts a sumptuous spectacle full of amazing dancers and her own classics. She's also proven to be a solid Vegas citizen, a staunch supporter of many important causes, and a work horse in ways that don't normally befit a star of her magnitude. Out gay director Brian Burke, a Franco Dragone protégé, has tweaked some of the more awkward moments out of the show and turned the spotlight on perhaps the most talented and sophisticated

dancing cast Las Vegas has ever seen. I still say there are times when I'm not sure Celine, who married her manager at a young age, understands the desperation imbued in songs like "My Heart Will Go On" and "I Drove All Night," but there's so much to look at with that huge stage and massive LED screen that it's not as distracting anymore. Plus, there are some unexpectedly homoerotic moments, most importantly when a mass of hot men writhe all over one another during "Seduces Me." Ostensibly, they're yearning for her, but they sure seem more intrigued by one another.

American Superstars

At Stratosphere

702/380-7777

Sun.–Tues. 7 p.m., Wed. and Fri. 8:30 p.m., Sat. 6:30 and 8:30 p.m.

Price: $38.75 for adults, $27.75 for children

BEEFCAKE-O-METER: 0 of 10

OVERALL QUALITY: F

Don't let the billing that this is the "ultimate celebrity tribute show" fool you. There's better in Vegas. Heck, there's better in Des Moines. The performers who do Tim McGraw, Elvis, and Britney Spears need new gigs.

An Evening at La Cage

At the Riviera

702/794-9433

Wed.–Mon. 7:30 p.m.

Price: Starts at $55

BEEFCAKE-O-METER:

OVERALL QUALITY: B+

This is the drag show that made drag safe for the mainstream. You'd expect *La Cage* to be a big gay draw—and sure, many gays go—but what's baffling and encouraging is that middle America fills the seats most nights. This is as wholesome as drag gets, what with Frank Marino doing his Joan Rivers bit and other men doing Diana Ross, Britney Spears, and Celine Dion. Jimmy Emerson, the courtly fellow who sends up Anna Nicole Smith and Madonna, is very clever.

Blue Man Group

At the Venetian

702/414-7469

Daily 7:30 p.m., Tues. and Sat. 10:30 p.m.

Price: Starts at $71.50

BEEFCAKE-O-METER: ⌐) ⌐)

OVERALL QUALITY: A-

Here's a genuine, off-beat, Las Vegas production show that happened to have been born somewhere else. Fortunately for all of us, it made it here after years in New York and other places that couldn't possibly understand them the way we, silly spectacle-loving Vegas audiences, do. The trio of Blue Men landed their custom-built showroom at the Venetian after five years at Luxor, but the show's pretty much the same—abstract comedy, noisy drumbeats, lots of Cap'n Crunch and Twinkee mush, and a finale in which the audience is covered with toilet paper. It's dopeyness dressed up as avant-garde artistry that's amusing nonetheless.

Carrot Top

At Luxor

702/262-4400

Sun., Mon. & Wed.–Fri., 8 p.m.; Sat. 7 and 9 p.m.

Price: $49.95

BEEFCAKE-O-METER: ⌐) ⌐) ⌐) ⌐) ⌐) ⌐) ⌐) ⌐) ⌐) ⌐)

OVERALL QUALITY: B+

Very beefy Scott Thompson uses his shaggy red mane, along with dozens of other goofy props, to make madcap, rapid-fire, physical

comedy. Thompson's intensely rocking physique is a slightly confusing but alluring twist on his performance, making the clown seem strangely sexy. He shows off his upper body twice in the show, once when doing a Michael Jackson scene in which his shirt is blown up by an air vent and once as Mick Jagger when the pecs are on display longer and less "accidentally." Plus, how can a gay man dislike a guy whose name is Mr. Top?

Crazy Girls

At the Riviera

702/794-9433

Wed.–Mon. 9:30 p.m.

Price: $34.95

BEEFCAKE-O-METER: 0 of 10

OVERALL QUALITY: B-

Any show that parades women fondling their breasts on a tiny stage to a song called "You Gotta Have Boobies" has to qualify for the "So Bad It's Good" award. This is a silly exercise in absurdest exploitation. It's also the one girlie show that's extremely welcoming to lesbians, marketing heavily in the gay media and not ignoring the babe-lusting babes when they come to drink and gawk. The dancing and music are ridiculous (real lyrics: "Girls, girls, crazy girls!"), but in a ultra-campy way that makes you, strangely, feel good.

Crazy Horse Paris

At MGM Grand

800/929-1111

Wed.–Mon., 8 and 10:30 p.m.

Price: $59

BEEFCAKE-O-METER: 0 of 10

OVERALL QUALITY: C

The reason *Crazy Girls, Jubliee!,* and *Folies Bergere* work—if that's the right word—is because they don't take themselves too seriously. When it's campy, it can be fun for gay men. But this nudie girly show—formerly called *La Femme* and changed for no evident reason other than perhaps a French title was too sophistique for Vegas horndogs—thinks of itself as high art when, in fact, it's a lot of very lithe, very naked women doing fancy dancing with rather serious lighting for a *lot* more money than it's worth.

Comedy Stop

At the Tropicana

800/829-9034

Daily at 8 and 10:30 p.m.

Price: $19.95

BEEFCAKE-O-METER: 🦵 🦵

OVERALL QUALITY: B+

For the price, this hit-or-miss comedy-variety lounge act is worth a try. Back when the Trop was a destination, bigger acts like Rosie O'Donnell would pop in, but today it's just a mixed bag of aspiring comics. What's great is that if one sucks, it's not long before he's gone and someone else is up there. Fair warning for gays, though: Some of the comics do homophobic routines. That's typical of low-brow comedians hoping to seem edgy, of course. Then again, some do homo-positive stuff. Don't take it personally, and don't be annoyed if the audience of frat boys eats up a little gay-baiting.

Danny Gans

At the Mirage

702/792-7777

Tues., Wed., Fri. and Sat., 8 p.m.

Price: $100

BEEFCAKE-O-METER:

OVERALL QUALITY: C+

What's scary about Danny Gans is not his uncanny ability to impersonate celebrities. It's the fact that his show hasn't changed much in a decade. The one-time minor-league baseball player is still telling O.J. Simpson and Bill Clinton jokes, believe it or not, and his NASCAR-Dad fan base eats it up. But, anyone with a mite of sophistication will just groan at most of the humor from a player who clearly is bored with his gig.

Jubilee!

At Bally's

877/374-7469

Sat.–Thurs., 7:30 and 10:30 p.m.

Price: Start at $65

BEEFCAKE-O-METER:

OVERALL QUALITY: B+

Funny how, were this a straight-male guidebook, I'd be lauding all the hot exposed breasts. Instead, it's that element of *Jubilee!*, along with the outlandish headdresses and cheesy production numbers, that makes this so amusingly campy for gay audiences. Here's a vintage Vegas show like they don't do anymore, preserved and presented for us as comedy instead of lewdness, plus some hot guys—many of them gay—cavorting to make it go down better. In that light, *Jubilee!* is well worth the time. As an added bonus, check out the backstage tours at 2 p.m. on Mondays, Wednesdays, and Saturdays. They're $15, $10 with the purchase of a show ticket.

Folies Bergere
At the Tropicana
702/739-2411
Sat., Mon., Wed., and Thurs., 7:30 and 10 p.m.; Tues. and Fri. 8:30 p.m.
Price: Starts at $64.90
BEEFCAKE-O-METER: 🦾🦾🦾🦾🦾🦾🦾🦾🦾
OVERALL QUALITY: B+

Along with *Jubilee!,* this is a relic of the days of the topless show-girls-with-big-feather-headdresses production shows. It's all so goofy—and that's precisely the point, so don't go in looking for Baryshnikov. For gay guys, some nice male bodies are on view. Plus, if the adorable emcee isn't a homeowner, then I'm a virgin.

George Wallace
At the Flamingo
702/733-3333
Tues.–Sat., 10 p.m.
Price: $59.95
BEEFCAKE-O-METER: 0 of 10
OVERALL QUALITY: C-

The good news is, comedian George Wallace doesn't bash gays. In fact, we don't figure into his down-home observational act at all. The bad news is, he's not funny. Wallace showcases a lot of humor that seems to play best with his African-American brothers and sisters who fill the room and love him, probably at least in part because he's the only black comic on the Strip. He seems to work hard, though, often sticking around for an extra half-hour when he likes the audience.

Gordie Brown

At the Venetian

866-641-7469

Tues., Fri., and Sat. 7:30 and 9:30 p.m., Sun. and Mon., 7:30 p.m.

BEEFCAKE-O-METER: 💪 💪 💪 💪 💪

OVERALL QUALITY: B

Vegas' newest headliner is vying for impressionist supremacy against the reigning mimic Danny Gans from directly across the street.

You can tell by Gordie's and Danny's respective energy levels—Danny sleepwalks, Gordie seems like he's on meth—who really wants to entertain and who wants a paycheck. All the standards are here—Jack Nicholson, George Bush, Robert De-Niro, Clint Eastwood—and for that Gordie gets a few demerits for predictability. But Gordie's standard-issue good looks are an excellent canvas for this sort of act and many of his impressions are dead-on.

GAY VEGAS

Lance Burton: Master Magician
At the Monte Carlo
702/730-7160
Wed.–Sat., 7 p.m.; Sat. 10 p.m.
Price: Starts at $66.50
BEEFCAKE-O-METER: 💪
OVERALL QUALITY: A

Even when Siegfried and Roy were around, Lance was the best magician in Vegas. He's not as campy or flashy and doesn't profit off of exotic animals. He just puts in an honest night's work making stuff disappear and reappear, with a great deal of square humor. Gay couples with kids would be remiss not to check him out.

Le Rêve
At Wynn Las Vegas
702/770-9966
Thurs.–Mon., 7:30 and 10:30 p.m.
Price: Starts at $79
BEEFCAKE-O-METER: 💪💪💪💪💪💪💪💪💪💪
OVERALL QUALITY: B-

This aquatic spectacle from Franco Dragone, who created *Mystère*, *O*, and Celine's *A New Day …*, bathes you in visions of perfectly sculpted, always wet men in nothing but brown brief-trunks. In that way, this show is hotter than any of the male revues. And there are sequences that portray same-sex intimacy between

both men and women that seem genuine, not exploitative. Yet there's also an ongoing gag about a clown's infatuation with one of the studs and much attempted humor found in dressing him in a pink tutu. Worse, though, is that the show has one of the most expensive minimum ticket in Vegas and it amounts, sadly, to a cheap knock-off of *O, Mystère,* and *Zumanity.* The acrobatics are redundant and the show itself relies too heavily on the impressiveness of the showroom. An overhaul of this show is to be completed in the summer of 2007 by openly gay director Brian Burke, who says he'll be enhancing some of the light effects and altering the narrative dramatically.

LOVE

At the Mirage
702/963-9634
Thurs.–Mon., 7 and 10 p.m.
Price: Starts at $69
BEEFCAKE-O-METER: ꒰ ꒰ ꒰ ꒰ ꒰
OVERALL QUALITY: A-

Even if you were never a huge fan of the Beatles, it's difficult not to admire and enjoy what Cirque du Soleil has done with the long-gone quartet in this imaginative replacement for *Siegfried & Roy.* Original Beatles producer George Martin and his son, Giles, digitized and remixed the actual Fab Four recordings to create a score that tells the story of pop music history's most successful band in Cirque-style allegories. The Mirage built a $120 million theater with splendorous acoustics that make you feel like the defunct band has reunited just for your Vegas audience. Many of the favorites are in here—"Lucy in the Sky With Diamonds," "Yesterday," "Help," "Sgt. Pepper's Lonely Hearts Club Band," and more—and another 100 or so were "represented" by a chord here or a drumbeat there. Cirque has traded in its over-the-top acrobatics for some very clever theater tricks, such as the piano filled with pink bubbles for "Strawberry Fields Forever" and an exploding Volkswagen in "A Day in the Life." As always, the costumes are vibrant, the performers are amazingly fit, and the theater itself is a stunning work of art. The one drawback is that, if you aren't familiar with some of the minutae of the Beatles legacy, you won't understand the significance of some of what you see. But then again, when did anyone understand the significance of what happens in a Cirque show?

Manilow: Music and Passion

At Las Vegas Hilton

702/732-5755

Tues.–Sat., 8 p.m. when in town

Price: Starts at $95

BEEFCAKE-O-METER: 0 of 10

OVERALL QUALITY: C

Manilow's arrival in Vegas was a rush job—and it shows. Next to nothing was invested in the production values, which leaves Barry crooning his song-book on a chintzy stage with dancers who seem confused about what they're doing. The closing number, "Copacabana," goes on and on. In fact, it may not be over yet. A mess, but somehow a very popular one.

O

At Bellagio

702/692-772

Wed.–Sun., 7:30 and 10:30 p.m.

Price: Starts at $102.85

BEEFCAKE-O-METER: ✊ ✊ ✊ ✊ ✊ ✊

OVERALL QUALITY: B

It's not that there's anything wrong with *O* exactly. It's got that amazing 1.5-million-gallon stage that can be deep enough for high-dives one minute and shallow enough for ballet. And the acrobatics and diving are superb. However, like that kid in school who always got straight A's, *O* gets boring after a while and its excellence is taken for granted. The water theme is both a blessing and a curse, allowing for a technologically remarkable experience while trapping the show in a series of redundant scenes. Still, there are some beautiful bodies to gaze at, which redeems it significantly.

Penn and Teller

At the Rio

702/777-7776

Sat.–Thurs., 9 p.m.

Price: $75

BEEFCAKE-O-METER: 0 of 10

OVERALL QUALITY: F

Let me be the only reviewer in Vegas to stand up and say I hate this show. Penn is a pompous ass and, through my dealings with him off-stage, I can say with certainty it's *not* an act. Teller's kinda fun, but Penn isn't and they fail to amaze the way Lance Burton does. What they're good at is self-promotion, which is how come you've heard of them ahead of several other magic acts in town. I admire self-promotion, but that doesn't mean I need to spend money to indulge it. Oh, and there's nothing of gay interest here, unless you think imagining Penn and Teller as a couple is hot. If so, that's just gross.

The Producers

At Paris Las Vegas

888/727-4758

Thurs.–Tues. at 8 p.m., and Sat. at 2 p.m.

Price: Starts at $75.50

BEEFCAKE-O-METER: 🦵 🦵 🦵 🦵

OVERALL QUALITY: A-

The latest Best Musical Tony winner to try its hand in Vegas arrived to very low expectations, what with the recent Vegas flops of *Hairspray* and *Avenue Q.* So nobody was more surprised than we were when we walked out pleased by this tres-campy tres-gay 90-minute version of Mel Brooks' classic. It's too bad that David Hasselhoff left so soon as the gay director Roger DeBris, but all in all, with openly gay Broadway vet and Tony nominee Brad Oscar as Max Bialystock, it's a solid production. That's not to say it'll be a big success in Vegas; it's still too reliant on its audience following the plot and lacks hit music (like *Mamma Mia!* and *Phantom*), two essential ingredients. And theater purists will be irked by the choppy cuts from the original, which reduce Ula to a brief burst of blond silliness rather than a full-formed character.

Rita Rudner

At Harrah's Las Vegas
Mon.–Sat., 8 p.m.
Price: $54
BEEFCAKE-O-METER: 0 of 10
OVERALL QUALITY: B+

Rudner's shtick is her brilliant observations on couples and their foibles, delivered with that cutesy lilt of a voice. Without a doubt, she's a scream. But she's nothing cutting edge or shocking and she doesn't do any gay humor of note. In fact, the peculiar thing about watching Rita's riffs about the male-female predicament with your partner will be realizing how such poles break down in same-sex relationships. For example: I'm the neurotic one (a female trait, says Rita), but I also hate to shop (a male trait, says she).

Second City Improv

At the Flamingo

702/733-3333

Fri., and Mon., 8 p.m.; Tues., Thurs., Sat., and Sun., 8 and 10 p.m.

Price: $39.95

BEEFCAKE-O-METER: ⌣ ⌣ ⌣ ⌣ ⌣

OVERALL QUALITY: A-

The famed improv Chicago troupe has a hilarious outpost in Vegas, sometimes with gay performers who occasionally bring in some very funny gay humor and some amusing fun-making about Vegas itself. As with any improv production, there will be disappointing nights, but for the price, and the reliability that something will work very well at least a few times an evening, it's a great deal.

Spamalot

At Wynn Las Vegas

702/770-9966; https://boxoffice.wynnlasvegas.com/spamalot.html

Sun., Mon., Wed. at 8 p.m.; Tues., Fri. and Sat. 7 p.m. and 10 p.m.

Price: Starts at $49

BEEFCAKE-O-METER: ⌣ ⌣ ⌣

OVERALL QUALITY: C-

If you or I had written this silly crap, it would never be staged, let alone become a Best Musical Tony winner on Broadway and then an attraction at a fancy Vegas resort. But since it's Eric Idle converting bits of his Monty Python canon and Mike Nichols staging it, somehow the smug New York theater media anointed it a hit. Granted, I'm not a fan of British comedy in general or Monty Python in particular, and there's a sort of cute gay subplot going on here in the form of a sort of closeted main character. But when grown men doing raspberries is considered high art, we're at a loss. Besides, this schlock replaced the brilliant *Avenue Q*, which had a similar gay subplot executed far better and with more of the sort of clever Broadway lyrics that would make Cole Porter grin.

Steve Wyrick: Real Magic

At Planet Hollywood

(702) 777-7794

Sat.-Thurs., 7 and 9 p.m.

Price: Starts at $69

BEEFCAKE-O-METER: 💪 💪 💪 💪

OVERALL QUALITY: C+

It's difficult to put your finger on exactly what's wrong with Steve Wyrick's "new" magic show in his eponymous $35 million theater complex. He does some excellent tricks, including one where he somehow interhooks three audience members' rings. But Wyrick, who's had gigs at at least two other properties before this one, is a puzzling performer for Vegas, acting as though there's a great deal of excitement and intrigue going on around him when really, there's not. He repeatedly attempts to get the audience excited by noting that this is "really big" magic and that the trick coming up "will keep you up tonight." No, not really. Some of the set pieces are cool, including a full-size small plane and a motorcycle. But Wyrick's voice is almost somnolent and though he's cute, he's also growing a bit paunchy (the clear outline of moobs were evident under his black shirt) and the act really hasn't changed all that much since the last time I saw him four years ago at the Sahara. In a town with Lance Burton already cornering the kiddie market and German illusionist Hans Klok due to open this summer with Pamela Anderson in tow to jack up the sex and camp appeal, there's no excuse for spending this kind of money on Wyrick.

Stomp Out Loud

At Planet Hollywood

(702) 785-5555; www.planethollywoodresort.com/stomp.php

Tues., Thurs.-Sun., 7 p.m.; Sat. 10 p.m.; Mon., 6 and 9 p.m.

Price: Starts at $50

BEEFCAKE-O-METER:

OVERALL QUALITY: B+

All I could think of watching this cast of 15 or so bang and beat on every conceivable household object—boxes, water bottles, trash cans, you name it—was: "A multi-ethnic array of beefcake." Indeed, the "music" is fine—OK, it gets a little grating after an hour, truth be told—and the performers work as hard as anyone in Vegas to entertain, but I was struck by how unusual it is to see rippled non-white men front and center in a Vegas production, in some cases shimmering under showers. While this production does not exactly succeed in recreating its New York original in a particularly new Vegas style, at least not as skillfully as *Phantom* does at the Venetian, it's still a whole lot of fun and what they're doing on stage looks easy but is, if you think on it, astonishingly difficult.

Toni Braxton: Revealed

At the Flamingo

800/221-7299

Tues.–Sat., 7:30 p.m.

Price: $65

BEEFCAKE-O-METER:

OVERALL QUALITY: B

The 1990s chanteuse's star has cooled, so she's decided to buff it up by playing in a sultry set in her own showroom she inherited from her idol, Gladys Knight. The original show was a bit disjointed and in some cases it was disturbing how she sort of lap-danced the audience,

MALE REVUES

The boom in all-male revues in Las Vegas signals a new open-mindedness— toward the *straight female* tourist. They aren't, however, intended for, or even particularly friendly to, gay men, who typically won't be seated up close and will never be invited to slide dollar bills into the G-strings of the boys involved. At last count, three major all-male stripper shows occupied stages at major Strip hotels: *Chippendales: The Show* at the Rio (8:30 p.m. Thurs.–Tue., 10:30 p.m. Fri.–Sat.; tickets start at $39.95, 702/777-7776); *Thunder From Down Under* at the Excalibur (9 p.m. nightly, 11 p.m. on Fri.–Sat.; $39.95. 702/597-7600); and *American Storm* at the Riviera (10:30 p.m. Tue.–Sun., $49.95, 877/892-7469). They're all the same tired routine of highly muscular men—frequently not particularly nice to look at above the chest—who appear as firemen or auto mechanics or whatever and boom-cha-boom, they're down to their skivvies.

The women are frequently with shrill bachelorette parties and resent the presence of gay men at least as much as many of the dancers seem to. That's not even the worst of it. After the shows are over, the lobby outside is crowded with horny straight men who didn't attend, but who stand outside waiting, wishing, and hoping to score with the sex-starved female showgoers after the guys on stage get them all moist.

Two of the major strip clubs, Olympic Gardens and Sapphire, also have male re-vues. But Olympic Gardens *prohibits* men from coming to see the show unless ac-companied by a woman. Sapphire has no such policy and the purveyors say they welcome gay male patrons, though male-on-male lap dances are disallowed. The owner told us he sees the potential for a gay side to the biz, but that he can't find any openly gay dancers to service that popula-tion. He also said he won't advertise in GLBT publications, because he fears the show will become tainted as a gay attraction. Hmm.

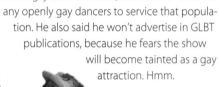

Bottom line: Head over to Gipsy or Krāve where you're more than wel-come to stuff the boys' pants with your fortune.

but that's been toned down a bit and her voice is in fine form. All the favorites that made her a gay icon are here, from "Breathe Again" and "Unbreak My Heart" to "Seven Whole Days." Plus, she dishes out the beefcake generously with some pipin' hot backup dancers.

Tournament of Kings
At the Excalibur
702/597-7600
Wed.–Mon. 6 and 8:30 p.m.
Price: $58.24
BEEFCAKE-O-METER: 💪 💪 💪 💪 💪 💪 💪 💪
OVERALL QUALITY: A-

OK, so here's an oddity—a show intended for little kids that provides loads of hot studs, sometimes shirtless, for appreciative adults to enjoy. This dinner-theater production is set in the Camelot age and involves some nonsense about warring factions, an effort to kill the king, blah blah blah. Just enjoy watching beautiful men on beautiful horses doing equestrian stunts and getting dirty and sweaty. And hurry up, too. Word is this show will be replaced by a Cirque du Soleil production by decade's end. Fair warning, though: The food is utterly bland.

Zumanity

At New York-New York

702/740-6815

Wed.–Sun. 7:30 and 10:30 p.m.

Price; Starts at $75.80

BEEFCAKE-O-METER:

OVERALL QUALITY: B

Cirque du Soleil's attempt to be daring and risqué is a mixed bag. Gay audiences must tip their hats to Cirque for the sequence in which a gay male couple does a ballet that climaxes with an intense, minute-long, male-male kiss. That alone makes the $50 million show the most expensive production to include overt male homosexual content to be staged for mainstream audiences. But Joey Arias, the legendary New York City drag queen, (see Q&A, page 129) is horribly wasted with tired embarrassing lines and an awful segment in which he leads the audience in a fake orgasm. How 7th grade. Plus, the female kissing in the fishbowl is exploitative lesbianism for straight male consumption.

Q & A with Frank Marino

Any drag queen who gets sued by the woman he impersonates is clearly doing something right. Yet Frank Marino, 41 (frankmarino.com), has done more than just survive a lawsuit filed by Joan Rivers; his uncanny aping of her has turned him into the longest-running headliner on the Strip. The self-styled Queen of Las Vegas has helmed *An Evening at La Cage* at the Riviera for more than 20 years and 20,000 shows now and in 2005 he was the second to receive a star on the Las Vegas Celebrity Walk of Fame. He's also appeared on countless TV talk shows and such movies as *Miss Congeniality 2*. Not surprisingly, all this success has led to naysayers and public spats.

Q: How do you respond to people who question your talent and criticize your acumen for self-promotion?

A: I don't. I believe there's room for everyone on the Strip. It's unfortunate that some people are jealous of me, but it goes with the territory.

Q: How do other performers on the Strip from other shows take you?

A: I get along with ninety-nine percent of the Strip performers. I feel like Sammy Davis, Jr. in the Rat Pack back in the day. The others will enter in the front door; I still take the back door. I'm among them, but I'm not one of them. I don't know if that's because I'm a gay performer or a drag performer or what.

Q: How did your drag career start?

A: Well, I was going to school in New York City and planning to be a doctor and I was doing drag in nightclubs at the time. I got a reputation for my Joan Rivers. Then I saw Joan in Atlantic City and went backstage and she was so impressed that she introduced me to the producers of a drag show called *La Cage*. I got a job with the show in Florida, and then Pia Zadora saw it in Florida and brought the show to Las Vegas.

Q: Has the format been the same for 20 years?

A: Yes, I come out as Joan and then as Frank Marino in drag between the superstars. But we change the show with the times. We used to do Ann-Margret and Julie Andrews. Now it's JLo and Britney.

Q: What makes a good candidate?

A: Everybody has to know them. There are a lot of stars that aren't well enough known. We need stars that are universal. We wouldn't use, for example, Christina Aguilera, because if I asked grandmothers at the mall who she was, they wouldn't know. But they'd know Britney Spears, because she's so notorious beyond her music.

Q: Are your audiences mostly gay?

A: Oh no. I think it's a very small segment. Night after night, it's Middle America in those seats.

Q: What do you think of the gay community here?

A: It's touch and go. It's such a transient city. There's never anybody here long enough to make a difference. Well, there are some people. And I've seen a five hundred percent change. But certainly there's a long ways to go.

GAY N**6**GHTLIFE

One reason Las Vegas gets a bad rap among gay travelers is that the gay nightlife resembles that of a much smaller city. A mere 15 bars for a community of 1.6 million people that greets 38 million tourists a year? Pathetic by any count. And the fact that not a single one of those bars is geared primarily to lesbians is especially galling.

That said, on any night of the week, gay men and lesbians have a bunch of choices. Those dozen or so bars do, after all, span a remarkable diversity of interests, from the fuzzy-sweater preppy crowd to the chaps-wearing country line dancers.

I. COMMERCIAL CENTER

Badlands Saloon (953 E. Sahara Ave., 702/792-9262): Here's a bar for folks who really like Western kitsch, starting with the faux Old West-saloon facade. And behind the bar resides a peculiar collection of ceramic cattle wind chimes. Seriously. Regular patrons, typically of the over-30 furry variety, even get cubbyholes for their own

personalized beer mugs. There's a down-home feel here that's incredibly comforting, right down to the 25-cent pool table. Fittingly, the Nevada Gay Rodeo Association hosts a $5 beer-bust fundraiser here the fourth Saturday of each month with line dancing. Video poker. No cover. Open 24/7.

Las Vegas Lounge (900 E. Karen Ave., 702/737-9350): A surprisingly large, surprisingly nice club that caters to transgender people, transvestites, and their admirers. Note that many men in the club are actually straight, both among the crossdressers and their suitors. Video poker, dancing, shows, and video games. No cover. Open 24/7.

Ramrod (900 E. Karen Ave., Ste. H-102, 702/735-0885): A standard gay club with the requisite bar, dance floor, darts, video poker, and pool table, which urges patrons to come and cruise with a daily calendar of events that includes the "best rump" contest. Two-for-one happy hours 4-8 p.m. daily. No cover. Open 24/7.

Spotlight Lounge (957 E. Sahara Ave., 702/696-0202): The standard-bearer in Vegas for the neighborhood gay bar, the Spotlight is owned by queer elder statesman Jack Novick, who avails the place to any charity that asks and is always first in line to sponsor GLBT and HIV/AIDS causes. There's nothing frilly about the joint; a jukebox plays shit-kicking country and rock, the air and carpet are soaked in smoke, the snaky bar is one of those places where everyone wants to chat, and the beer is always cheap. The crowd tends to be older. No cover. Open 24/7.

II. THE FRUIT LOOP

This bar corridor about a mile east of the Strip and a mile north of the airport is so named for its circuitous traffic pattern. The gay developers of the area started calling it that in jest, but never came up with anything else and it stuck. Despite the potential offensiveness of the moniker, even the local newspapers occasionally use it and nobody much minds. Here are the bars in this cluster.

The Buffalo (4640 Paradise Rd., Ste. 11, 702/733-8355): A smoky tavern for the Levi/leather crowd with video poker, pool tables, darts, and music videos. It's popular among both tourists and locals for its low-key atmosphere, especially compared to the attitude that prevails at stand-and-pose Gipsy. No cover. Open 24/7.

Free Zone (610 E. Naples Dr., 702/794-2300; www.freezonelv. com): This all-purpose nightclub has with a large dance floor that's

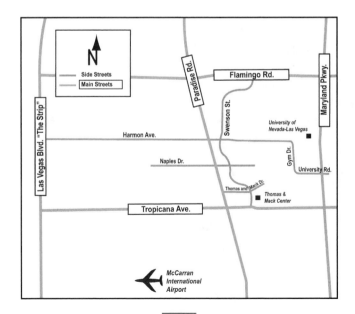

crammed on the weekends, when 10 p.m. drag shows bring out raucous crowds. Drink specials are frequent, particularly during the 4–8 p.m. daily happy hours, when all well drinks are just a buck. Video poker. Restaurant open daily 6 p.m.–2 a.m. with chicken wings, burgers, etc. Web site offers free e-mail newsletter. No cover. Open 24/7.

Gipsy (4605 Paradise Rd., 702/731-1919; www.gipsylv.net): The most opulent dance club in Las Vegas is also an old perennial that's stood the test of time. The Gipsy consists of a large central dance floor playing club favorites and showing off go-go boys; a quieter bar room is partitioned by colorful glass. Gipsy tends to attract the stand-and-pose crowd, the hotties with attitude, as well as those just looking for good dance beats. Cover charges vary, none on some nights. Free valet parking. Open daily 9 p.m. to early morning.

Piranha/8½ Ultra Lounge (4633 Paradise Rd., 702/290-3583; www.gipsylv.net): Spending a whopping $4.3 million, the owners of Gipsy and Suede have outdone themselves by building what is easily one of the nation's most elegant gay bar/lounges. Celebrities agree; Britney Spears and Janet Jackson have both been spotted here. All that money really did buy a transformative experience, a club with plush banquets and booths, flat-panel TVs, and earth-tone stonework. The two-in-one-club concept works, allowing loungers to enjoy the relative quiet and elegance of 8½, while hard-driving partiers can jam to music in the huge room past the piranha-filled aquariums.

In the Piranha area, a two-bottle minimum and a reservation earn an upstairs private booth with leather couches and suede-paneled walls from which to stare down at the dance floor. Plus, there's an outdoor patio with gas-burning fireplaces and waterfalls, depending on the season. Both open 9 p.m. nightly. Cover charges apply on certain nights and times.

Suede Restaurant & Lounge (4640 S. Paradise Rd., 702/791-3463): This corner spot, in a former incarnation, was the gay club where the Killers got their start. The redesign is pretty, with purple-suede banquets and crystal chandeliers, plus serviceable and inexpensive food. It's a quieter spot amid the tumult of this bar district, except when there's live music or other entertainment. No cover. Open Tues.–Sun., 6 p.m.–9 a.m.

III. ONE-OFF WONDERS

Backdoor Lounge (1415 E. Charleston Ave., 702/385-2018): The Backdoor markets to Hispanics and is in a Hispanic neighborhood about two miles east of downtown. Parking and entry are confusing; patrons must go to the rear to enter. Once inside, though, it's a large space with a pretty aquarium, a fireplace, a dance floor, and a performance stage for live entertainment. The bathrooms are a little cruisy, with a peephole in one stall wall, and the place tends to draw lots of guys in cowboy hats. Video poker, pool table, dancing, and shows. Cover is $5 on Friday and Saturdays after 9 p.m. Open 24/7.

Barcode (5150 Spring Mountain Rd., 702/221-5150): This new addition to the bar scene is a much-needed industrial-style dance club with black padded-vinyl walls and plush banquets. Everything here, though, focuses on the dance floor, a spacious rectangle below an imposing stage where drag and other shows take place regularly. There's also an upstairs area to perch and watch the dance-floor action. Pool table, wi-fi, minor hot-snack service, and daily 2-for-1 drink happy hour 4–9 p.m.

Charlie's Las Vegas (5012 S. Arville, 702/876-1844; www.charlies lasvegas.com): Among the greatest surprises in the Vegas gay scene is this country-western bar where attitude is checked at the door and the music is actually low enough to converse with friends. The Sunday-night beer-bust tea dance is a local gay-community ritual that attracts even those repulsed by standard-issue gay bars, with line-dancing lessons and a $5 beer bust. Afterwards, many folks walk over to the café at the Orleans Hotel-Casino for dinner. Thursday nights around 8 p.m. are busy here, too. Formerly the Backstreet Saloon, it was acquired by a chain that operates similar venues in Denver, Phoenix, and Chicago. Open 24/7.

Escape Lounge (4213 W. Sahara Ave., 702/364-1167; www. escape loungelv.com/Home.html): From the same folks who brought us Goodtimes over in the Liberace shopping center comes this local gay sports bar about four miles west of the Strip. This is a much better and cleaner option than Flex, which is in the same neighborhood. Escape has darts, pool and table-shuffleboard, plus food from 4 p.m. to midnight daily. Granted, the menu is loaded with artery-clogging fried options. Daily two-for-one happy hour 5–7 a.m. and 5–7 p.m. Video poker. Open 24/7.

Flex (4371 W. Charleston Blvd., 702/385-3539; www.flexlasvegas. com): A small squalid corner club about six miles northwest of the Strip, Flex hops after midnight on Saturdays. The bathrooms are cruisy as the stalls have no locks. A friendly, if horny, locals crowd frequents the joint. No cover except after $5 on Saturdays after midnight. Video poker. Open 24/7.

Goodtimes (1775 E. Tropicana Ave., 702/736-9494; www.good timeslv.com/goodtimes.html): This formerly creepy little bar has spiffed up its act. Good thing, since it's 4,500 square feet of queer-bar space right next to the Liberace Museum, itself a Mecca for gay tourists. There are stripper and drag shows now, videos, a dance floor, and a digital reader that displays the names of the barbacks each day, a nice personalizing touch. Video poker. Pool. Wi-fi available. No cover. Open 24/7.

Hot Rods (3120 Sirius Lane, 702/873-5046): Just what Vegas needs, another underpopulated standard-issue bar, this time in a hard-to-find spot slightly west of the Strip. As this book goes to press, the owners opened this place without a liquor license and there was no video poker, food or pool. The best Hot Rods had to offer was stripper shows, but the lights go out when the towel is finally dropped. Open 24/7.

Krāve (3663 Las Vegas Blvd. S., 702/836-0830; www.kravelas vegas.com): The first bar on the Strip to cater directly to "alternative lifestyles"—they don't quite call it a gay bar, but they aggressively market to gays—is run by gays, has hot male go-go dancers, and hosts all sorts of gay and lesbian events. This is a mammoth and beautiful space at 17,000 square feet, two-thirds of which is a warehouse-style dance club with industrial club music and secluded booths. The other section is a quieter bar-lounge that, on certain nights, puts on specialty events. The club is attached to the Miracle Mile Mall, which is part of the Planet Hollywood Hotel-

Casino. But you can't get into the bar from inside the complex; you must walk outside to the Harmon Avenue entrance, which is dumb and confusing. From 5 to 9:30 p.m., the club uses its smaller bar area for Lucky Cheng's Drag Cabaret Restaurant, a Vegas version of the irreverent New York Asian drag-queen dinner-theater concept in which patrons are serenaded, skewered, and served by off-the-wall cross-dressers ($69.95 per person includes the entertainment and a three-course meal; 702/836-0836). Krāve is also the only gay club in town with a dress code, however loose, that prohibits baggy jeans, cutoffs, sandals, or baseball hats. And, much to their credit, they aggressively market to lesbians with weekly Saturday-night Girlbar events, produced by the L.A. duo who do this all over the country. Valet parking on Harmon Avenue. Open 11 p.m. to 3 a.m. weeknights, 10 p.m.-6 a.m. on Friday and Saturday. Cover is $10 for members, $20 for non-members, except on certain nights.

Las Vegas Eagle (3430 E. Tropicana Ave., 702/458-8662): Like every other city, Vegas has an Eagle, a smoky joint catering to men who love hair and leather—and the men who love them. This one's about three miles east of the Fruit Loop, tucked into a strip mall that also includes a bank and several ethnic restaurants. Video poker. No cover. Open 24/7.

Snick's Place (1402 S. Third St., 702/385-9298; www.snicksplace. com): Las Vegas' longest-open gay bar—it turned 30 in 2006—is a cute downtown Las Vegas locals establishment with cheap drinks and a big-screen TV on which "Monday Night Football" is shown by ritual. On the side of the building is an elaborate gay mural painted by the

community in 2005 as part of the Las Vegas Centennial Committee's murals program. Fair warning: The neighborhood's a little creepy. Video poker, pool. No cover. Open 24/7.

B. GAY-FRIENDLY NIGHTSPOTS

Ghostbar (at the Palms, 702/942-6832): For a sensational view of the city, there are few offerings quite like this low-key old favorite. The space has hosted several gay fundraisers. Also, there's that wicked glass floor on the deck that hangs about 50 stories over the ground. Opens 8 p.m. nightly.

Lure (at Wynn Las Vegas, 702/770-3633): When the Wynn's advertising agency started taking out full-page ads for Lure with women in suggestive poses under a tagline "Attraction Has No Rules," many thought it might be a gay lounge. It's not, but it is a sleek comfortable spot with gauzy white-fabric draping, mirrors, and candlelight, where gay couples are extremely welcome to drink and romance. Word is they may be renaming the club later in 2007. Cover charge Wednesday is $10, Friday and Saturday $20, free other nights. Women always free. Open daily 10 p.m.–4 a.m., closes at 5 a.m. Friday and Saturday.

OPM (inside Forum Shops, 702/369-4998): While this 8,000-square-foot club's attempt at a weekly gay event, Shampoo Saturdays, failed due to lack of interest and/or promotion, it's a testament to the Wolfgang Puck-owned hotspot's interest in gay clubbers. OPM sits atop Puck's Chinois eatery and the Asian influences are omnipresent in the décor and even the employees' uniforms. Puck provides an after-hours menu of sushi, dim sum, and desserts. The music is unadulterated funk and progressive beats. Cover $10 on Wed.–Thurs., $20 Fri.–Sun., Open Wed.–Sun. 10 p.m.–6 a.m.

Playboy Club/Moon Nightclub (at the Palms, 702/942-6832): Yes, it's Playboy. But if Playboy stands for anything these days, it's live and let live. The Palms reclaims its recently lost position at the head of the Sin City nightlife pack with this unique two-in-one ultralounge and dance club connected by escalators and a uniform cover charge on the 52nd and 53rd floors of the new Fantasy Tower. The lower level is the sleek Playboy Club, the Hefners' first attempt at reviving and updating a franchise that went out of business in late 1980s by greeting patrons—who do not need membership keys for admission as they did in days of old—with a très-Vegas Playboy sign made of 10,000 diamond-shaped crystals and bunnies in new Roberto Cavalli-designed ears and cottontails. There's also a casino, the only one in Nevada with a cover charge for entry, but this Playboy Club is a largely subdued dim-lit affair with music soft enough to converse over and bottle service available at large, wide, plush leather banquettes along the floor-to-ceiling windows. For a more energetic experience, there's the upper-level 12,500-square-foot Moon Nightclub with the only retractable roof over a dance floor in at least North America. Cover is $20-$40 depending on the day. Open 8 p.m. nightly.

Pure (inside Caesars Palace, 702/212-8806; www.purethe nightclub.com): Used to be, Vegas nightclub impresarios believed the best way to get a good view of the Strip from their

clubs was to plop the club atop a hotel tower. Pure broke that mold with a stunning 14,000-square-foot open-air terrace jutting out along the famed byway. The deck itself is eye-popping, too, with cascading waterfalls, walls of fire, leather-upholstered private cabanas, and a massive dance floor. Such gold-plated investors as Celine Dion, André Agassi, Steffi Graf, and Shaquille O'Neal made sure Pure redefined Vegas chic in every conceivable way, including ensuring that on any given weekend, some of their A-list celeb pals would be around, from the Hiltons to the Simpsons. Gay couples feel right at home being affectionate and dancing close, both on the deck and on oversized beds scattered around the main indoor dance floor. Cover is $20. Open Fri.–Sun., and Tues. from 10 p.m.–4 a.m.

Tabu (inside MGM Grand, 702/891-7183; www.tabulv.com): Of the many ultralounges in Vegas nowadays, this one is truly transporting and astonishing. Tabu has two tabletops that sport projected images on them that actually react to human motion; wave your hand over parts of it and the image will actually move and change! Really! Even if you haven't been drinking! Gay travelers will enjoy the very accepting naughty atmosphere that

includes tabletop dancing, models as waitresses, and the occasional celebrity drop-in. Cover charges are $20 Tues. to Thurs., $25 Fri.–Sat. Open Tues.–Sun. 10 p.m. to dawn.

Rain in the Desert (inside the Palms, 702/942-7777): This is a now-legendary 25,000-square-foot nightclub with a bamboo dance floor surrounded by fountains and mist. Another one of the celeb-set's favorites, it's also known for a hot male staff, some of whom are openly gay. Music is mostly hip-hop, dance, old-school, and rock. Cover $10 Thurs., $25 Fri.–Sat. No cover for local women. Open Thurs.–Sat. 11 p.m.–5 a.m.

Studio 54 (inside the MGM Grand, 702/891-7254; www.studio 54lv.com): Las Vegas reinvented the famed New York City dance club

that once drew Andy Warhol and his posse as a party headquarters for everyone, straight and gay, with both male and female go-go dancers. Like at the original, classic-movie iconography abounds, with black-and-white photos of celebrities everywhere. Confetti cannons and balloon drops heighten the festivities, as do the acrobats hanging from the ceiling. If nothing else, Studio 54 earns its place on this list by hosting the annual Beaux Arts Ball, a no-holds-barred Halloween party that benefits Golden Rainbow, one of Vegas' best HIV/AIDS charities. Cover $10 Tues.–Thurs.; $20 Fri.–Sat.; Ladies free. Open Tues.-Sat. 10 p.m.–dawn.

Q & A with Joey Arias

As a drag legend in Greenwich Village, Joey Arias (joeyarias.com) toiled on the edge of respectability for decades. The Fayetteville, N.C., native ran with Andy Warhol and friends in the 1970s and 1980s and built an iconic stature of his own that led to performances at Carnegie Hall and a regular column in *Paper* magazine. But he largely left all that behind in 2003 to emcee Cirque du Soleil's bawdy production *Zumanity* (see page 113) trading in the coolest of queer addresses for Vegas, a city that caters largely to Middle America. And yet, in bringing his naughtiness to that crowd, he feels he's turning an act in which he wears Thierry Mugler gowns and carries a bullwhip mike into a form of social progress.

Q: What is Zumanity's *significance to Vegas?*

A: It's historic. Landmark. *Zumanity* is a great springboard for showing America all the varieties of sexuality. It was a little shocking when we opened. Some people walked out. But Cirque knew what it was doing and now people are comfortable with it. I mean, it's the twenty-first century. If you can't see two men kiss, c'mon. It's important that I'm on the Strip and that this gay culture is out there. I am a national treasure.

Q: How gay a city is Vegas?

A: To me, the city is very gay, starting with the names of the streets—Flamingo, Paradise, Howard Hughes. They all sound so queer.

Q: Do your high-brow friends think it's tacky?

A: Oh no. They think it's amazing. Two artist friends from Germany came to visit and they thought Vegas was like a sculpture. They didn't think it was real. They saw the Eiffel Tower, the New York-New York, the pyramid at Luxor and thought it was art for art's sake.

Q: Is Las Vegas real?

A: Oh, yes. Las Vegas is real for what it is. It's more genuine than other places, because it's based on gambling, tits and ass, and it's completely unapologetic about that.

Q: What's been your most surreal gay experience here?

A: Finding these bars here are so from the 1960s. You wouldn't see some of these places in New York anymore, a place like Snick's Place (see page 124). That's something that should've gotten ripped down a long time ago. I mean, their logo is a pink elephant. That's just surreal.

Q: The gay bar scene is behind the times?

A: The gay scene here is evolving, but it's not evolved at all. In New York or other big cities, they're really crazy, fun, out of control. Here they're a little uptight still.

Q: You said when you arrived here in 2003, two years and out. Why are you still here?

A: I'm not done with the city yet. I'm still seeing changes and they're treating me well, so I keep going. All my friends from all over the world are going, "Wow, you're one of the lucky ones because you're working. Make your money." That's what I'm doing.

Q: Celebrities come by the show all the time, don't they?

A: Oh God, yes. Rene Russo came backstage the other night and she spotted me and she said, "You're so fucking great." And gave me a big fucking hug.

WEEKLY ACTIVITIES

This calendar is subject to change, but only the most consistent events are listed.

Sunday

Badlands Saloon: $3.50 beer bust 9 p.m. to midnight.

Barcode: Two-for-one drinks 3–9 p.m., drag show 11 p.m.–midnight.

Blue Moon Resort: Free cookout at pool with $15 day-pass entry.

The Buffalo: $5 beer bust 4–7 p.m.

Charlie's: $5 beer bust 4–7 p.m. $2 Long Island iced teas 7–midnight.

8½-Piranha: $2 well/draft 9–11 p.m. $10 liquor bust. No cover.

Escape Lounge: Two-for-one drinks 5–7 a.m. and 5–7 p.m.

Flex: $1 drinks 4–8 p.m.

Free Zone: Free pool and karaoke. $1 well/draft drinks 4–8 p.m., beer bust 8 p.m.–1 a.m.

Gipsy: Illusions Cabaret Show at 10:30 p.m. and 1:30 a.m.

Goodtimes: Two-for-one well/domestic drafts 5–7 p.m.

Las Vegas Lounge: Transgender go-go dancers at 10 p.m.

Ramrod: "Ram or Be Rammed" tea dance, beer and liquor bust noon to 4 p.m.

Snick's Place: $1.50 well drinks and domestic beer 2–4 p.m. and 2–4 a.m.

Suede: $2 drinks 6–7 p.m. and 10 p.m.-midnight.

Mondays

Badlands Saloon: Two-for-one domestic and well drafts 4–7 p.m.

Barcode: Two-for-one drinks 4–9 p.m., live mic starts 10 p.m.

Charlie's: Cuervo Blue Martinis $1.50 and dance lessons 7–9 p.m.

8½-Piranha: $2 well/draft 9–11 p.m. $10 liquor bust. No cover.

Escape Lounge: Two-for-one drinks 5–7 a.m. and 5–7 p.m.

Flex: Free pool and raffles, $1 drink specials 4–10 p.m.

Free Zone: Free pool and karaoke starting at 9 p.m. Go-go boys. $8 liquor bust. $1 well/draft drinks 4-8 p.m., free beer bust with call-shot purchase 8 p.m.–1 a.m.

Gipsy: Latin Night and $5 beer bust 9 p.m.–1 a.m.

Goodtimes: $15 liquor bust 11 p.m.–4 a.m. Two-for-one well/domestic drafts 5–7 p.m.

WEEKLY ACTIVITIES (CONT'D)

Kräve: No cover, $10 all-you-can-drink. Opens at 10 p.m.

Las Vegas Lounge: Transgender go-go dancers at 10 p.m.

Ramrod: Strip contest at 11 p.m.

Snick's Place: $1.50 well drinks and domestic beer 2–4 p.m. and 2–4 a.m.

Suede: $2 drinks 6–7 p.m. and 10 p.m.–midnight

Tuesdays

Backdoor: Video night, drink specials from midnight to 8 a.m.

Badlands Saloon: Two-for-one domestic/well drinks 4–7 p.m.

Barcode: Two-for-one drinks 4–9 p.m.; Asian night starts at 10 p.m.

The Buffalo: $5 beer bust 9 p.m. to midnight. Bear Chest contest last Tuesday.

Charlie's: Two-for-one Bud Light 7 p.m.–midnight.

8½-Piranha: Hip-hop night; free Bud Light bust with shot purchase 11 p.m.–2 a.m. No cover. $2 well/draft 9–11 p.m.

Escape Lounge: Two-for-one drinks 5–7 a.m. and 5–7 p.m.

Flex: Amateur variety show starting after 10 p.m. Male strippers at midnight. $1 drinks 4–8 p.m.

Free Zone: Ladies night, women go-go dancers. Wet T-shirt contest second Tuesday of the month. $1 well/draft drinks 4–8 p.m., beer bust 8 p.m.–1 a.m.

Goodtimes: Two-for-one well/domestic drafts 5–7 p.m.

Kräve: Latino night includes drag show. Two-for-one drinks 11–midnight. No cover 11 p.m.–midnight.

Las Vegas Lounge: Transgender go-go dancers at 10 p.m.

Ramrod: Beer and liquor bust 9 p.m.–1 a.m.

Snick's Place: $1.50 well drinks and domestic beer 2–4 p.m. and 2–4 a.m.

Suede: $2 drinks 6–7 p.m. and 10 p.m.–midnight; two-for-one dinners, $2 appetizers and movies shown on plasma TVs.

Wednesdays

Backdoor Lounge: Two-for-one well drinks and draft beers 4–6 p.m.

Badlands Saloon: Two-for-one domestic beers and well drinks 4–7 p.m.

Barcode: Two-for-one drinks 4–9 p.m., hip-hop night starts at 10 p.m.

WEEKLY ACTIVITIES (CONT'D)

Charlie's: $1 mini-pitchers all day.

8½-Piranha: Ladies' night with go-go girls. Free Bud Light bust with shot purchase 11 p.m.–2 a.m. $2 well/draft 9–11 p.m. $5 cover after 9:30 p.m.

Escape Lounge: Two-for-one drinks 5–7 a.m. and 5–7 p.m.

Flex: Latin music night. Free raffles, $10 liquor bust starting at 10 p.m. $1 drinks, 4–8 p.m.

Free Zone: $1 well/draft drinks 4-8 p.m., $8 liquor bust and $4 beer bust 8 p.m.–1 a.m. with call-shot purchase.

Gipsy: Retro music night.

Goodtimes: Two-for-one well/domestic drafts 5–7 p.m.

Krāve: Boy Heaven amateur go-go boy contest starts at 11 p.m. $100 prize for winner. $2 well drinks, $5 call drinks, no cover.

Las Vegas Eagle: Underwear night 10 p.m.–3 a.m. Free well and draft if you wear just underwear.

Las Vegas Lounge: Transgender go-go dancers at 10 p.m.

Ramrod: Beer and liquor bust 9 p.m.–1 a.m.

Sin City Q Social: Weekly Martini Mixers at 8 p.m. at various bars. See www.sincity qsocials.com for upcoming locations.

Snick's Place: $1.50 well drinks and domestic beer 2–4 p.m. and 2–4 a.m.

Suede: $2 well drinks at 6–7 p.m. and $1 draft at 10 p.m.–midnight.

Thursdays

Backdoor Lounge: Two-for-one well drinks and draft beers 4–6 p.m.

Badlands Saloon: Two-for-one domestic beers and well drinks 4–7 p.m.

Barcode: Two-for-one drinks from 4–9 p.m., Latino Night starts at 10 p.m., $2 Tecate all night. Two-for-one well drinks 10 p.m.–1 a.m.

Charlie's: Line dancing lessons 7–9 p.m. Two-for-one drinks 7 p.m.–2 a.m.

8½-Piranha: Go-go boys, bartenders wear briefs. $5 Bud Light bust or free with shot purchase 11 p.m.–2 a.m., $2 well/draft, 9–11 p.m. No cover.

Escape Lounge: Two-for-one drinks 5–7 a.m. and 5–7 p.m.

Flex: Poker tournament starts at 10 p.m. $1 drinks 4–8 p.m.

Free Zone: Boys Night with go-go boys starts 11 p.m. $1 well/draft drinks 4–8 p.m., beer bust 8 p.m.–1 a.m.

WEEKLY ACTIVITIES (CONT'D)

Gipsy: Seduction drag show at 2:30 a.m.

Goodtimes: Military appreciation night. $10 liquor bust 10 p.m.–2 a.m. with military ID. Two-for-one well/domestic drafts 5–7 p.m.

Krāve: Hip-hop night, $2 well/Smirnoff drinks, $5 call drinks. Opens 11 p.m.

Las Vegas Lounge: Transgender go-go dancers at 10 p.m.

Ramrod: Best Buns Contest at 11 p.m.

Snick's Place: $1.50 well drinks and domestic beer 2–4 p.m. and 2–4 a.m.

Suede: $2 well drinks at 6–7 p.m. and $1 draft at 10 p.m.–midnight; karaoke 10 p.m.–2 a.m.

The Center: Free anonymous HIV/AIDS and syphilis tests and free hepatitis A and B inoculations 3–6:30 p.m.

Fridays

Backdoor Lounge: Latin Seduction Night.

Badlands Saloon: Liquor bust, $5, 7 p.m.–midnight

Barcode: $5 VanGogh vodka martinis 4–9 p.m.

The Buffalo: $5 beer bust 9 p.m.–1 a.m.

Charlie's: 75-cent drinks and two-step lessons 7–9 p.m.

8½-Piranha: $2 well/draft drinks 9–11 p.m. No cover.

Escape Lounge: Two-for-one drinks 5–7 a.m. and 5–7 p.m.

Flex: Drag revue at 10 p.m. $1 drinks 4–8 p.m.

Free Zone: Martini Mixer business social with two-for-one martinis 5–9 p.m. Drag show at 10 p.m. $1 well/draft drinks 4–8 p.m., beer bust 8 p.m.–1 a.m.

Gipsy: Go-go boys, $5 beer bust 11 p.m.–2 a.m., drag show at 1 a.m.

Goodtimes: Dance floor opens at 10 p.m. Two-for-one well/domestic drafts 5–7 p.m.

Krāve: $2 drinks 11–midnight, $5 thereafter. Open 11 p.m.–5 a.m. $20 cover for non-members.

Las Vegas Eagle: Underwear night 10 p.m.–3 a.m. Free well and draft if you wear just underwear.

Las Vegas Lounge: Transgender go-go dancers at 10 p.m.

Ramrod: Free drinks for shirtless men and best-chest contest at 11 p.m.

WEEKLY ACTIVITIES (CONT'D)

Snick's Place: $1.50 well drinks and domestic beer 2–4 p.m. and 2–4 a.m.

Suede: $2 well drinks 6–7 p.m. and $1 draft at 10 p.m.–midnight; two-for-one dinner specials 6–8 p.m.; karaoke 10:30 p.m.–2:30 a.m.

Saturdays

Backdoor Lounge: "Gelmis & Her Girls," a drag show, at midnight.

Badlands Saloon: Beer bust, $5, 7 p.m.–midnight (benefits NGRA fourth Saturday of the month).

Barcode: Two-for-one drinks 4-9 p.m.

Charlie's: 75¢ drinks and two-step lessons 7-9 p.m. Plus, at 7 p.m. on every third Saturday, patrons born that month get free cocktails.

8½-Piranha: $2 well/draft drinks 9–11 p.m. $5 cover.

Escape Lounge: Two-for-one drinks 5–7 a.m. and 5–7 p.m.

Flex: Hip hop/urban music after midnight. $1 drinks, 4–8 p.m.

Free Zone: Drag show at 10 p.m. $1 well/draft drinks 4–8 p.m., beer bust 4-8 p.m.

Gipsy: Go-go boys, $5 beer bust 11 p.m.–2 a.m., drag show at 1 a.m.

Goodtimes: Dance floor opens at 10 p.m. Two-for-one well/domestic drafts 5–7 p.m.

Krāve: Girlbar 9 p.m.–3 a.m. in lounge; Everything You Desire party with go-go boys 11 p.m. in main bar. Afterhours party starts at 3 a.m.

Las Vegas Eagle: Underwear night 10 p.m.–3 a.m. Free well and draft if you wear just underwear.

Las Vegas Lounge: Transgender go-go dancers at 10 p.m.

Ramrod: Drag show at 11 p.m.

Snick's Place: Beer bust, $5, and liquor bust, $6, from 9 p.m.–midnight; $1.50 well drinks and domestic beer, 2–4 p.m. and 2–4 a.m.

Suede: $2 well drinks from 6–7 p.m. and $1 draft at 10 p.m.–midnight; two-for-one dinner specials 6–8 p.m.; karaoke 10:30 p.m.–2:30 a.m.

VEGAS' M7ST PHALLIC

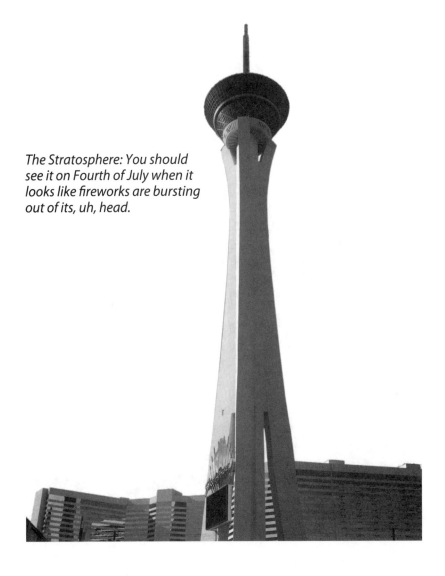

The Stratosphere: You should see it on Fourth of July when it looks like fireworks are bursting out of its, uh, head.

Bellagio Dancing Fountains: Particularly that last deafening burst shooting high in the air.

Pink's hot dogs at the Planet Hollywood: Where 12 inches is not an exaggeration.

Yard-long drinks shaped like the Eiffel Tower: Fun to watch Midwest frat boys with their mouths on the ends of these.

The name says it all, doesn't it?

Deep-fried Twinkies on Fremont Street: The white stuff fills your mouth.

The light shooting out of the Luxor: Talk about drama queens.

80-foot retractable runway at Fashion Show Mall: Cute boys and girls go up and down, up and down.

UNLV Flashlight: A monument to the student, uh, body.

Fremont Street Experience: Light and sound as far as the eye can see.

SPAS

Las Vegas is all about commotion and noise. From the advertising cacophony greeting you at baggage claim to the lights flashing in your window at all hours, moments of peace are about as rare as hitting a royal flush on a video poker machine. The one place to truly escape the ruckus is the spa. No wonder, then, that as the destination goes high end, some hotels are putting some muscle into this once-ignored side of the resort biz. Note below that in some cases, spa access is restricted to hotel guests.

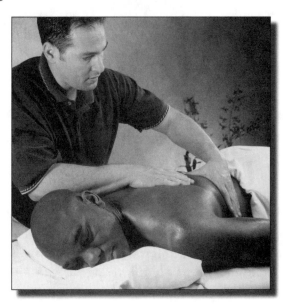

Bathhouse Spa

At THEhotel at Mandalay Bay

877/632-9636

Hours: 6 a.m.–8:30 p.m.

Basic 50-minute massage $125 plus tip

Don't be deceived; this is not some sleazy sex center, despite the lurid name. It's actually one of Vegas' best-designed spas, optimizing a comparatively modest 14,000 square feet. The Bathhouse is appointed with suede walls, marble floors, and ubiquitous streams and waterfalls, and offers a remarkable array of inventive touches, such as the questionnaire to answer from which they create a personally tailored blend for massages. Another fun feature: You can watch your own little TV with earbuds during pedicures.

Canyon Ranch SpaClub

Inside the Venetian Hotel-Casino

877/220-2688

Hours: 5:30 a.m.–10 p.m.; must be a hotel guest for access

Basic 50-minute massage $140 weekdays, $150 weekends, plus tip

At 69,000 fabulous and transportative square feet, Vegas' version of the Canyon Ranch franchise is not just the largest here, but among the biggest in North America. This is the spa as it ought to be, with both first-class treatments and a terrific restaurant with "healthy-gourmet" cuisine to recover at. Among the 62 treatment rooms is the Rasul chamber, an oval room where a single or a couple can sit in body masks for herbal steaming. When the treatment's over, the ersatz night sky above starts to rain.

The Grand Spa

At the MGM Grand Hotel-Casino

702/891-3077

Hours: 6 a.m.–8 p.m., non-guests charged $5 more per service and not permitted Fri. and Sat.

Basic 50-minute massage $130 plus tip

Probably the most gay-friendly of the city's spas, if only because the staff enthusiastically embraces same-sex couples who come in for the two-hour Couples Dream Ritual. That treatment starts with a foot soak, then a full-body exfoliation and scalp treatment, then an Aboriginal massage, before the couple slink off into the shower to wash one another off. Otherwise, the spa itself is pretty standard, a 29,000-square-foot space with 20 treatment rooms.

Hibiscus Spa

Inside the Westin Casuarina Hotel & Spa

702/836-9775

Hours: 6:30 a.m.–8 p.m. Sun.–Wed., 6:30 a.m.–9 p.m. Thurs.–Sat.

Basic 50-minute massage $115 plus tip

A smaller low-key offering that's more affordable, the Westin's 10,000-square-foot spa with 15 treatment rooms offers the basics, plus a few creative touches, like a treatment that concludes with warm coconut milk poured over the body.

Qua Baths and Spa

Inside Caesars Palace

866/782-0655

Hours: 6 a.m.–8 p.m.

Basic 50-minute massage
$140 plus tip

Caesars Palace pretty much ignored the high-end spa trend that exploded in the past decade, but now with innovative and beautiful Qua, they're poised to make a play for a business it largely ceded to Bellagio and the Venetian. Qua is a 50,000-square-foot complex appointed with tan stonework, dark wood paneling, and ubiquitous waterfalls that denote the name-implying aquatic theme. The conceit is evidenced everywhere, from the dramatic single-sex Roman Baths boasting several overflowing pools of differing temperatures to four different styles of sauna, including an Arctic Room that cools guests off with a nippy breeze and white snow-like foam flowing from the ceiling. Among Qua's other innovations is the tea sommelier who offers waiting or lounging guests 19 brew varieties that range from highly caffeinated (the "Golden Assam" mix) to tranquil-inducing (try "Summer Rain"). Qua also is the only spa in Vegas to offer an artist who applies Swarovski Crystal body images wherever the client would like.

Spa Bellagio
702/693-7111
Hours: 6 a.m.–8 p.m. Must be a hotel guest for access
Basic 50-minute massage $130 plus tip

As with everything else at Bellagio, this spa is the quintessence of beauty and service. A recent doubling in size to 65,000 square feet and 56 treatment rooms means the addition of such novelties as a room for Watsu, an Asian massage that takes place in a jacuzzi, and a 1,000-square-foot Bamboo room that features Pilates and kickboxing lessons. Also notable is the Egyptian Gold Body Treatment, an exfoliation and massage that conclude with dusting the face with real gold.

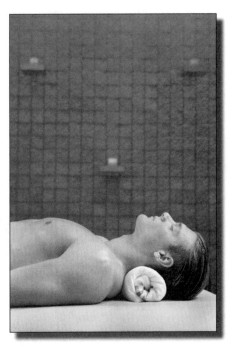

The Spa at Green Valley Ranch Resort & Spa
At Green Valley Ranch; 702/617-7570
Hours: 6 a.m.–8 p.m.
Basic 50-minute massage $140 plus tip

A true getaway from the Vegas hullabaloo is this 60,000-square-foot spa at this elegant property 10 miles southeast of the Strip. Killer views of the Strip abound from the yoga room. The specialty is the Grand Deluxe Package, which includes a 50-minute Swedish massage, an almond and peaches facial, carrot-cake body therapy, pedicure, and hair wash and style.

The Spa at Red Rock Casino, Resort & Spa

702/797-7878

Hours: 6 a.m.–8 p.m.

Basic 50-minute massage $140 plus tip

The 35,000-square-foot spa at Vegas' newest megaresort—and sister property to Green Valley Ranch—is appointed in the same red earthtones as the rest of the place and the namesake mountains that loom besides it. A 23-page spa directory offers more than a hundred facials and massage choices, but what's more interesting is the Adventure Spa menu that includes horseback riding and hikes in historic state parks nearby. Plus, in a Vegas novelty, there's even a private outdoor swimming pool for spa users.

The Spa at Wynn Las Vegas

702/770-3900

Hours: 6 a.m.–8 p.m. Must be a hotel guest for access.

Basic 50-minute massage $145 plus tip

Given the grandeur that marks the Wynn resort, it's surprising that the 35,000-square-foot spa is so simple and obligatory. It's bathed in an oppressive red and consists pretty much solely of two long hallways lined with its 45 treatment rooms. The menu is similarly ordinary.

SHOPPING 9

Yet another requirement for admission into the pantheon of world-class vacation destinations is providing so many top-brand shops that even the most devoted browser will eventually be sated. That surely wasn't Vegas a decade ago, when a dice clock was about as fancy a souvenir as you'd come by.

Nowadays, Sin City understands the powerful allure of Cartier, Tiffany, and Nordstrom. Even Barneys will be here by the end of 2007 at the Palazzo, the new tower at Venetian. But for gay shoppers looking for more, uh, utilitarian items, there's plenty of that, too.

A. THE STRIP

Forum Shops

At Caesars Palace

702/ 893-4800; www.caesarspalace.com

160 shops, 13 restaurants

Hours: Sun.–Thurs., 10 a.m.–11 p.m.; Fri.–Sat., 10 a.m.–midnight

Grade: A++

Far and away the marquee shopping experience in Las Vegas, the Forum

Shops is one of the most profitable malls in the world as measured by sales per square foot. It's no wonder. The expansion in 2004 added a startling 175,000 more square feet, as well as a breathtaking atrium under which shoppers ride spiral escalators to three levels. Highlights among the 160 shops include the CH Carolina Herrera (which has men's clothes, too), Anthropologie, Louis Vuitton, Kiehl's, Harry Winston, Fendi, Dior, Juicy, Niketown, and the world's largest Peter Max Gallery. Caesars also managed to keep one of only a few FAO Schwarz toy stores in America after the company folded, a bi-level store with a huge Trojan Horse in front. There are also some amazing places to eat even if you're not interested in shopping, from Wolfgang Puck's Chinois to Joe's Seafood, Prime Steak & Stone Crab.

Fashion Show Mall

3200 Las Vegas Blvd. S.

702/369-0704; www.thefashionshow.com

250 stores and restaurants

Hours: Mon.-Fri., 10 a.m.–9 p.m.; Sat., 10 a.m.–8 p.m.; Sun., 11 a.m.–6 p.m.

Grade: A-

Don't be put off by the ridiculous spaceship-looking disc looming over the place; the Fashion Show's recent redesign has vastly improved its inside look and offerings. The department stores alone are an impressive collection that include Vegas' only Nordstrom, Saks Fifth Avenue, and Apple stores, as well as Williams-Sonoma, Bang & Olufsen, and Lucky Brand. As for food, there's an 11,288-square-foot food court with seating for—gasp—1,500, as well as the delicious Capital Grille, Café Ba-

Ba-Reeba, and California Pizza Kitchen. This is probably the only mall you'll ever go to that is *not* dominated by teenagers, so enjoy that. And in addition to the normal people-watching that such shopping centers are notorious for, the Fashion Show—true to its moniker—holds fashion shows every half-hour on an 80-foot retractable runway outside the Apple store starting at 1:30 p.m. Mon.–Sat. and 12:30 p.m. on Sundays. Often, the models, both male and female, show off bathing suits. Yum.

Grand Canal Shoppes

At the Venetian

702/414-4500; www.venetian.com

Hours: Sun.–Thurs., 10 a.m.–11:00 p.m., Fri.–Sat., 10 a.m.–midnight

Grade: B+

The keys to the Grand Canal Shoppes are the Grand Canal and the rest of the Venetian atmospherics, from the painted frescoes on the ceilings to the street performers that include wandering jugglers and opera trios. This is, by far, the most tranquil and transcendent setting in all of Vegas shopping, making for a calm stroll with the Italian arias of the gondoliers hanging in the air. The shopping line-up, however, fails to rise to the exclusive levels of Via Bellagio or the Forum Shops: The solid but not stunning lineup includes Jimmy Choo, Aldo, and Sephora. The mall is, however, a primo dining destination, featuring Tao, Tsunami Asian Grill, and Wolfgang Puck's Postrio.

Las Vegas Premium Outlets

875 S. Grand Central Pkwy

702/474-7500; www.premiumoutlets.com/lasvegas

120 stores

Hours: Mon.–Sat. 10 a.m.–9 p.m., Sun. 10 a.m.–8 p.m.

Grade: A-

Bargain shopping has never felt quite this upscale. The Premium

Outlets, located about three miles north of the Strip, is a 435,000-square-foot outdoor mall with names you almost never find at these sorts of places—Banana Republic, Bose, and Crabtree & Evelyn among them. Other high-end names like Ann Taylor, Dolce & Gabbana, and Kenneth Cole offer out-of-season or out-of-style wares for as much as half off. And unlike most other off-Strip attractions, plenty of cabs await to haul you and your haul back whence you came.

Mandalay Place

Bridge between Luxor and Mandalay Bay

www.mandalayplace.com

41 shops and restaurants

Hours: Sun.–Thurs. 10 a.m.–11 p.m., and Fri.–Sat. 10 a.m.–12 a.m.

Grade: C-

A lackluster shopping experience is rescued by the presence of a few funky vendors—Urban Outfitters, Chocolate Swan, and the Strip's only really cool bookstore, the Reading Room. The marquee here, however, is a shop called 55 Degrees Wine + Design, owned by the former wine guru of Charlie Palmer's Aureole and designed with the same futuristic panache as Aureole, which includes a chilled wine-rack room

and innovative glassware. Restaurant RM, Rick Moonen's seafood joint (see review, page 73), is among the best fishhouses in town. That said, Mandalay Place isn't a shopping destination so much as worthy of a quick browse if you're in the vicinity.

Miracle Mile Mall

At Planet Hollywood

888/800-8284. www.desertpassage.com

170 stores, 16 restaurants

Hours: Sun.–Thurs., 10 a.m.–11 p.m., Fri. and Sat., 10 a.m.–midnight

Grade: B

The Miracle Mile, formerly known as Desert Passage, is one of my partner's favorites, so it's worth noting that they do have major outposts of fcuk, Sephora, and Aldo, among others. The trouble is, just like everything else at this ill-conceived edifice, it's hard to get in and out—it's easiest to come in from the parking garage—and it's a dizzying circle that never leads anywhere.

Via Bellagio

At the Bellagio

702/693-7111; www.bellagio.com

27 shops, 19 restaurants

Hours: Daily 10 a.m.–midnight

Grade: A-

While the Forum Shops was first to offer true high-end shops, it is managed separately from Caesars Palace and looks very little like the rest of the property. Via Bellagio, then, was a revolution in integration, affording shoppers the same beautiful floral carpeting, color scheme, and ornate lighting, so as to not take you out of your Bellagio experience. The result is a Rodeo Drive-style experience that remains among the most important stops on the Vegas trail. Tiffany & Co., Hermes of Paris, and Prada are all exclusively at Bellagio. When you and your charge cards are worn out, refresh at Café Gelato.

Wynn Esplanade

At Wynn Las Vegas

702/770-7000; www.wynnlasvegas.com

27 stores

Hours: Sun.–Thurs., 10 a.m.–11 p.m.; Fri.–Sat., 10 a.m.–midnight

Grade: B+

If any part of the Wynn Las Vegas could be mistaken for Bellagio, it's the shopping arcade. There you'll see Chanel and Dior, just like at that other little joint Steve Wynn built down the block. But you'll remember where you are when you see Wynn's name on not one, not two, but four different shops. Still, there are some novelties, mainly Graff jewelers, Manolo Blahnik, and Oscar de la Renta, not to mention the Penske-Wynn Ferrari-Maserati dealership, although that's on the other side of the casino. Plus, there may be two other Louis Vuitton stores on the Strip, but neither has a marquee as big, bold, and fittingly Vegas-sized as the one at Wynn.

B. GAY-RELATED SHOPPING

I. SPOTLIGHT

Get Booked
4640 Paradise Rd., #15
702/737-7780; www.getbooked.com
Hours: Mon.–Thurs. 10 a.m.–midnight, Fri.–Sun. 10 a.m.–2 a.m.

Smack-dab in the heart of the Fruit Loop bar area, just a mile east of the Strip, is this venerable Vegas institution, the gay bookstore Get Booked. In addition to the usual fiction and non-fiction books, Get Booked also carries a respectable collection of queer-related DVDs and other knick-knacks. When gay authors come to town, they tend to do readings and signings here. Among other things, this is your one-stop shop for picking up all the region's GLBT publications and I mean all; this is a distribution point for free papers from Reno, Phoenix, and L.A. They also carry all the gay tchotkes you'd want from one of these places, including clubwear, gag gifts, rainbow stickers, and pornographic magazines.

II. OTHER GAY STUFF

Artspace Gallery (1400 S. Third St., 702/636-1800): A funky art, furniture, and antique gallery in downtown Las Vegas next to the gay bar Snick's Place staffed by volunteers of the Nevada AIDS Project, whose profits go to that charity. Some of the furniture is donated cast-offs from displays at the nearby World Market Center.

Bare Essentials, Fantasy Fashions (4029 W. Sahara Ave., 702/247-4711; www.bareessentialsvegas.com): The tagline in its ads goes, "Where entertainers, dancers, producers ... everyone shops!" They sell leather thongs, clubwear, sex toys, wigs, and a huge selection of G-strings for men. Open Mon.-Sat., 10 a.m.–7 p.m., Sun. noon–5 p.m.

Leather Addictions (700 E. Naples Dr. #103, 702/558-2223; www.leatheraddictions.com): Buy men's and women's leather clothes or rent portable slings and other BDSM accoutrements. Open Mon.–Thurs. noon–10 p.m., Fri.–Sat., noon-midnight, Sun. noon–5 p.m.

The Male Bag Vegas (610 E. Sahara Ave. #13, 702/474-6253; www.the malebagvegas.com): The Bag offers a variety of male clubwear, plus DVDs, lube, and sexy underwear. Open Mon.–Sat., 10 a.m.–8 p.m.; Sun. 10 a.m.–6 p.m.

Price Video (700 E. Naples, 702/374-1342): This video store in the Fruit Loop, right next to 8½ and Gipsy, has all the mainstream movies and a large gay porn collection. Open daily 10 a.m.–10 p.m.

The Rack (953 E. Sahara Ave. #16, 702/732-7225): In Commercial Center. Browse the vast collection of fetish wear, club clothes, and sex toys and visit the theater, called the Onyx (see page 167), in back. Open 10 a.m.–9 p.m. Sun.-Thurs., 10 a.m.–midnight Fri.-Saturday.

CUL**10**RE

Sin City gets a pretty bad rap when it comes to arts and culture. It's true, there's no MOMA or Art Institute here, no cute art-house movie theaters to speak of, and precious few independent coffee houses beyond ReJavaNate Coffee Lounge (see page 65). Still, there are options—and more than you'd expect.

A. MUSEUMS

Atomic Testing Museum

755 E. Flamingo Rd.

Las Vegas, NV 89119

702/794-5151; www.atomictestingmuseum.org

Price: $10; $7 for seniors, military and kids 7–17, free for children under 7

Hours: Mon.–Sat., 9 a.m.–5 p.m., Sun., 1–5 p.m.

Only in Vegas would a serious museum offer a thrill ride and a ton of atomic camp. At this institution a mile east of the Strip, visitors get a simulation of what it was like in the 1950s and 1960s to sit out in the desert and watch an above-ground nuclear test—complete with trembling benches and blasts of air—inside the Ground Zero Theater. One of the nation's first museums to focus on Cold War history, this $3.5 million collection recalls the 928 nuclear tests that took place from

1951 to 1992 in the Nevada desert and examines their role in winning the Cold War. Ignored, however, is the plight of thousands poisoned by radioactive residue in the process. The kitsch factor is high here, with 1950s postcards and pictures of mushroom clouds, not to mention all the wacky stuff (Einstein dolls!) for sale in the gift shop.

Bellagio Gallery of Fine Art
At Bellagio
877/957-9777; www.bgfa.biz
Price: $15, $12 for Nevada residents, students and seniors
Hours: Daily 9 a.m.–10 p.m.

Back in 1998, it was impressive enough for art-starved Vegas to have this gallery full of the private pieces of Steve Wynn. But the real art revolution arrived in Vegas after his company was bought out by what became MGM Mirage and he exited with his collection. That's when Bellagio brought in Pace Wildenstein, the biggest art dealer in New York City, to put on amazing, highly curated, and intelligent shows. Since then, the Pace folks have used their influence and respect to bring collections of Monet, Fabergé, and Warhol to the property, often putting on shows that include pieces never seen before in North America. It's not a large space—about 1,600 square feet, good for 30 to 50 pieces of art—but that's enough for the ADHD-afflicted Vegas visitor. Exhibitions change every few months and are always worth a visit.

Donna Beam Fine Art Gallery
At University of Nevada-Las Vegas
4505 S. Maryland Pkwy.
Las Vegas, NV 89154
702/895-3893; finearts.unlv.edu/Facilities/Donna_Beam_Gallery
Price: Free
Hours: Mon.–Fri. 9 a.m.–5 p.m. and Sat. 10 a.m.–2 p.m.

A respectable offering from the local university has frequently changing exhibits from up-and-coming artists and middling stars. Nothing too earth-shattering here, but it's a good reason to go wander the campus while you're at it.

Guggenheim Hermitage
At the Venetian
702/414-2440; www.guggenheimlasvegas.org
Price: $19.50, $15 for seniors and Nevadans, $12.50 for students, $9.50 for children 6-12
Hours: Daily 9:30 a.m.–7:30 p.m.

Following the Wynn-Bellagio lead, two of the art world's most prestigious forces—the Hermitage Museum in St. Petersburg, Russia, and the Solomon R. Guggenheim Foundation in New York—teamed up to create this impressive space at the Venetian. In recent years, they've hosted beautiful collections from Rubens, Warhol, Rothko, and Renoir, although it earns

its respect from the GLBT crowd for its daring Robert Mapplethorpe exhibit late in 2006. It's a larger space than Bellagio's and the audio narration is about as solid, but it's also a bit more expensive and the gallery, while designed by Pritzker Prize-winning Dutch architect Rem Koolhaas, isn't really that interesting to look at.

Las Vegas Art Museum

9600 W. Sahara Ave.

Las Vegas, NV 89117

702/360-8000, www.lasvegasartmuseum.org

Price: $6, $5 for seniors, $3 for students, free for children under 12

Hours: Tues.–Sat. 10 a.m.–5 p.m., Sun. 1–5 p.m.

OK, so it's no Louvre. But the Las Vegas Art Museum, thanks to its affiliation with the Smithsonian Institution, frequently brings in fascinating exhibits by both revered and up-and-coming artists. Housed in a main branch of the local library system about 10 miles west of the Strip on Sahara Avenue, the LVAM has almost monumental walls on which hang exhibits from oversized-canvas maestros like Chinese-American painter Marlene Tseng Yu.

Liberace Museum

1775 E. Tropicana

Las Vegas, NV 89119

702/798-5595; liberace.org

Price: $12.50, $8.50 for seniors and students, children under 6 free

Hours: Tues.–Sat., 10 a.m.–5 p.m.; Sun. noon–4 p.m.

Once painfully tacky, this tribute to the famed pianist who practically invented over-the-top Vegas camp was recently renovated into a respectable and seriously curated presentation. Three miles east of the Strip on Tropicana Avenue, guests wander from room to room learning about the Liberace legend and the role that rhinestone-encrusted

grand pianos and 50-pound feather costumes played in creating it. Check out the rare Moser crystal; the only other identical set in the world is owned by Queen Elizabeth II. Openly gay pianist Wes Winters performs a Liberace tribute show Wed., Thurs., and Sat. at 1 p.m. and costs $14.95. Fair warning, though: The restaurant once owned by Liberace, Carlucci's Tivoli Gardens, is a shadow of its former high-society self, a sad and limp little Italian eatery next door that merely trades on its old Liberace links.

Lied Discovery Children's Museum

833 Las Vegas Blvd. N.

702/382-3445; www.ldcm.org

Price: $8, $7 for children

Hours: Tues.–Sat., 10 a.m.–5 p.m., Sun. noon–5 p.m.

Believe it or not, there's more for kids to do in Vegas than casino arcades and roller coasters. About 10 miles north of the Strip, this excellent children's museum has lots of hands-on offerings, such as the faux grocery store where they must pick out items and stay within a budget. Beyond that, there's usually a little Vegas pizzazz here, too, like the 2005 exhibit called "Neon Unplugged" that explained just how the city gets its famous sparkle.

Neon Museum

702/387-6366, neonmuseum.org

Price: $5 per person for guided tours of 10 or more, $50 total for smaller groups

Hours: By appointment only on weekdays

Full disclosure: The so-called Neon Museum is not a pretty sight. Two junkyards about seven miles north of the Strip known collectively as "The Boneyard" are crammed with more than 100 pieces of non-operational—but still fabulous—signage. As fearsome as that may sound, the Neon Museum provides an up-close-and-personal look at an only-in-Vegas sort of history. Among the mountains of metal and broken bulbs are letters from the old Stardust sign and the 20-foot high-heeled shoe that once revolved atop the Silver Slipper's marquee. The folks who run the museum hope to have a proper site open to all in coming years and recently acquired the old Googie-era clamshell-shaped lobby of the La Concha Motel for its future visitors center. For now, visitors can only see the collection on appointment-only group tours. (Anyone can pay the $50 for a private individual tour, too.) Eleven of the classic signs, including such iconic entries as the Hacienda Horse and Rider, are restored and functioning on the public plaza of the Fremont Street Experience.

B. THEATER

Nicholas Horn Theatre (3200 E. Cheyenne Ave., North Las Vegas, 702/651-4052; www.ccsn.edu/pac): A community theater that's part of the Community College of Southern Nevada, the Horn Theatre presents plays and concerts almost every weekend. Past performances have included *Macbeth*, Eugene O'Neill's *Thirst and Fog,* and Stephen King's *Misery,* as well as jazz and choral concerts.

Boulder Theatre (1225 Arizona St., Boulder City, 702/293-5001): Once a quaint movie house for this quiet town 30 miles southeast of the Strip, it's now owned by Desi Arnaz Jr., who restored the nearly 75-year-old structure. It's presently home to the Boulder City Ballet Company.

Clark County Library District Film Series (various libraries around town, www.lvccld.org/events/movie_series.cfm): The local library district routinely offers up cutting-edge films—including gay ones like *Aimee and Jaeger* and *Torch Song Trilogy*—through its film series. Usually, they're free.

Egg and I Dinner Theater (4533 W. Sahara Ave., 702/616-3322; www.eggandi.com): This cute, popular, breakfast place two miles west of the Strip is known both for large egg dishes at reasonable prices ($7-$8 a person) and for its unusual habit of turning into a dinner theater four nights a week. *Marriage Can Be Murder*, an audience-participation comedy murder mystery that changes every two months, is performed Wed.-Fri. at 7 p.m. and Sat. at 6. Guests can choose from chicken, salmon, and pasta entrées, which aren't quite as good as breakfast, but the shows are always intriguing and often funny. It's not cheap, but the $60/pp cost includes the show and dinner and two-for-one coupons appear frequently in the *Las Vegas Review-Journal, Las Vegas CityLife,* and *Las Vegas Weekly.* Also, reservations by phone avoid online ticket-broker handling fees. Most guests take cabs from the Strip, but it's important to ask the restaurant to summon one back, as it's not easy to grab one on the streets in off-Strip areas of Vegas. Note: This is not affiliated with the Egg & I chain that has locations all over Colorado and in Utah.

Las Vegas Academy of International Studies, Performing and Visual Arts (315 S. 7th St., 702/799-7800; www.lvacademytheatre.org): Some of the gutsiest theater in Vegas is going on at the magnet high school for the performing arts, where in 2004 the school was picketed by the virulently anti-gay Rev. Fred Phelps for putting on *The Laramie Project.*

Las Vegas Little Theatre (3920 Schiff Dr., 702/362-7996; www. lvlt.org): This struggling but worthy small theater company frequently stages gay shows, from *Making Porn* to *Take Me Out.*

Las Vegas Philharmonic (performs at Ham Hall at UNLV and in private homes, 702/258-5438; www.lasvegasphilharmonic.com): The Phil offers a full schedule of orchestra events, most intriguingly the Connoisseur Series that showcases stars of the troupe in small concerts in the homes of Phil benefactors.

Nevada Ballet Theatre (performs at the Performing Arts Center at UNLV, 702/243-2623; www.nevadaballet.com): Yes, some professional dancers in Vegas are not strippers or Celine back-ups! This 35-member company includes dancers recruited from around the world. To show the community is serious about its ballet, the NBT received a huge grant in 1996 to build its current 36,000-square-foot facility for rehearsing and administration.

Nevada Conservatory Theatre (at UNLV, 702/895-3663; nct.unlv. edu): The gay *Las Vegas Review-Journal* theater critic Anthony Del

Valle raves, "If I were to recommend one Vegas theater to subscribe to, it would be the NCT." Frequently, the NCT puts on challenging material, among the recent examples being the cancer play *Wit*.

Onyx Theater (in the back of The Rack, 953 E. Sahara Ave., #16, 702/732-7225): Many were dubious when The Rack owners, who also own the Hawks bathhouse, opened this 100-seat theater, figuring it would be a porn venue. Instead, it's turned out to be a place to screen obscure gay films, to stage plays like *Torch Song Trilogy*, and for twice-monthly dress-up shows of *The Rocky Horror Picture Show* (first and third Saturdays of the month at 11:30 p.m.).

Performing Arts Center (on the UNLV campus, 702/895-2787; pac.unlv.edu): A collection of three venues, the Ham Concert Hall, the Judy Bayley Theater, and the Black Box Theater, are home to a list of local lecture and concert series that have brought such names as Wynton Marsalis, Bebe Neuwirth, Bob Woodward, Itzhak Perlman, Aaron Copland, and many others to the valley. The Nevada Conservatory Theatre and UNLV Orchestra are just two of the entities that use these spaces. Check the Web site's calendar for the latest.

Regal Village Square Cinemas (9400 W. Sahara Rd., 800/326-3264): The only multiplex in Las Vegas that shows art-house flicks and small independent movies, from *Mysterious Skin* to *An Inconvenient Truth*.

Super Summer Theatre (at Spring Mountain Ranch State Park off Charleston Blvd. about 15 miles west of the Strip, 702/594-7529; www.supersummertheatre.com): A theater-under-the-stars format from June to September with uber-family-friendly shows such as *Seussical the Musical* and *Tom Sawyer*. The setting is truly lovely, a big wide-open pasture at the foot of looming red mountains, although it's still pretty hot in the summer when the shows start at 8 p.m.

Thomas & Mack Center (4505 S. Maryland Pkwy., 702/739-FANS; www.thomasandmack.com): UNLV's arena is home to the school's Running Rebels basketball team, as well as host to innumerable concerts, boxing matches, and rodeos.

FIRST FRIDAY

One of the most delightful cultural developments in recent Sin City history was the 2002 advent of First Friday, a monthly four-hour crawl on—duh—the first Friday of each month, among some 50 galleries, restaurants, thrift shops, and other funky locales in downtown Las Vegas. Not surprisingly, it's become a must-do monthly event for queer Las Vegans; several local gay couples say they met at First Friday.

The event usually runs from 6 to 10 p.m., with a special free trolley that ferries attendees between nine stations in an area of about two square miles. Folks coming from the Strip should take taxis; cabbies do hang out around the Arts District area, so it shouldn't be too difficult to get back later.

Most attendees start their

FIRST FRIDAY (CONT'D)

evening at the Arts Factory (101 E. Charleston Blvd., 702/676-1111, www.thearts factory.com), a two-level artists colony that houses about 20 painters, architects, photographers, and others. It's the real hub of the First Friday action. Next door is the S2 Editions L'Atelier (1 E. Charleston Blvd., 702/868-7880, www.s2art.com), a super-cool 21,000-square-foot lithograph firm that boasts five of seven existing French-made 19th century Marinoni Virion presses. First Fridayers can watch the presses at work or browse prints from Todd Goldman, Al Hirschfeld, and Frank Sinatra, among others. After that, move along to Holsum Lofts (231-241 W. Charleston Blvd., 702/222-3022, www.holsumlofts.com), a 53-year-old former bread factory that's now home to several galleries and some commercial tenants. Then head to the Funk House (1228 S. Casino Center, 702/678-6278, www. thefunkhouselasvegas.com), a huge antique shop specializing in 1950s art glass, ceramics, and furniture. The Funk House is owned by Cindy Funkhouser, the pioneer who started First Friday in Oct. 2002. Several of her neighbors also are antique shops.

When you're hungry, there are several good options. The best of those is Tinoco's Bistro (103 E. Charleston Blvd., 702/464-5008), which is attached to the Arts Factory and is owned by longtime Las Vegas chef Enrique Tinoco. His salmon and Dungeness crab cakes are sumptuous and his prices—$10-$20 per entrée—are shockingly low. But it's the rustic motif with distressed hardwood floors, exposed pipes, and funky local artwork that makes it fit so well.

For a full map and up-to-date information on special events at upcoming First Fridays, visit www. firstfriday-las vegas.org or call 702/384-0092.

FUN WEDDINGS IN VEGAS

Even as the Nevada electorate stitched a same-sex marriage ban into the state constitution in 2002, Las Vegas hotels and attractions were opening some of their chapel doors to gay and lesbian couples to hold emotionally meaningful—if legally irrelevant—nuptials. Yes, that's right. You, too, can join in the tacky thrill of getting hitched in Vegas. And unlike Britney Spears, you won't need a team of lawyers to untangle you when you sober up.

That said, many independent wedding chapels in town don't do gay weddings. The Strip hotels that do them are denoted in the Lodging section of the book.

But here are some of the more exotic ways gays can be wed in Vegas:

• Fly to the bottom of the Grand Canyon and get wed with two guests, a minister, and a photographer for $2,695 through Sundance Helicopters. The fee includes a Webcast of the event for all your friends to watch (800/653-1881; www.helicoptour.com).

• Get married aboard the HMS *Britannica* surrounded by pirates and sirens on the lagoon at Treasure Island. It's also possible to have a pirate swing down on a rope from the crow's nest to hand off the wedding rings. The Enchantment package costs about $2,500 and includes a Swedish massage, manicure, hair and makeup (888/818-0999; www.treasureisland.com).

• Have Spock and Kirk attend your wedding on the bridge of the USS *Enterprise* at the Star Trek Experience at the Las Vegas Hilton. Several different packages are available, including the "Admiral's Wedding," which includes photography, a video, your choice of four Star Trek characters, and the display of a brass plaque at Quark's Bar and Restaurant recognizing your nuptials. You must BYOM (bring your own minister), but they discount you $100, so that package only costs about $2,900 (702/697-8750).

• If you can't go to gay Paris, then be gay at Paris Las Vegas—and get hitched atop the Eiffel Tower. The most elaborate package is the $10,000 Eiffel Tower at Twilight, which gets you the sunset-time ceremony, a two-night stay in a suite, Don Perignon in Waterford flutes, two hours of limo service, a 6- by 8-inch two-tier wedding cake, and a $500 Eiffel Tower Restaurant credit (877/650-5021; www.parislasvegas.com).

WYNN LAS VEGAS WEDDING CHAPEL

Q & A with Ron DeCar, Viva Las Vegas

Leave it to the only gay-owned wedding chapel in Las Vegas to also be among the most innovative and successful. At Viva Las Vegas, owned by longtime partners Ron DeCar and Jamie Richards, who met as Strip entertainers in the early 1990s, you choose from a variety of themed ceremonies, from an Elvis performing three songs for $275 to a *Phantom of the Opera* wedding in which the room is lit like the deformed opera-house spook's lair and Christine singing from a balcony for $750. DeCar, 48, is a former lead singer for *Folies Bergere* (see page 100), who started performing themed weddings on the side; Richards, 44, was a dancer in several Strip productions. Together they opened Viva Las Vegas (800/574-4450; www.vivalasvegas.com) in 1999, and business has been gangbusters ever since.

Q: VLV has always done gay weddings, but pretty much none of the other non-hotel chapels do. Why?

A: Some of the other independent chapels are affiliated with different religions or they don't have an interest in doing them. The hotels are more liberal because they know the gay market is out there and they want to cater to that. But at the same time, we're a place you can feel totally comfortable in and you can help a gay business succeed.

Q: Do you do a lot of same-sex weddings?

A: I'd say about 50 or 60 a month out of the 550 or so we do every month. That's a lot, really. Mostly they're lesbians. They're more apt to get married than the gay men.

Q: Which of your themed weddings do you think is the most fun?

A: Well, right now the Gothic weddings ($750) are pretty popular. What you get is that we do the chapel up in a foggy cemetery setting and I make an appearance rising out of the coffin. We have the minister dressed either as Dracula or the Grim Reaper.

Q: What ones do the gays go for most?

A: Actually, most of our gay or lesbian weddings are traditional. They're usually doing it for the first time, so they're not going to want to do themed wedding. Themed weddings, I think, are mostly for people who want to renew their vows.

Q: What celebrities have come to your chapel?

A: Erin Brokovich got married here and LeAnn Rimes came for a friend's wedding. Angelina Jolie was the maid of honor at the wedding of one "Judging Amy" co-star Jillian Armenante, who is a lesbian and married her partner.

Q: Are you and Jamie married?

A: Oh no. We wear rings and we're committed to each other, but we haven't had a ceremony. I think we're just around it too much.

GETTING 12 AWAY FROM THE STRIP

Ethel M Chocolate Factory and Botanical Cactus Gardens

1 Sunset Way, Henderson

702-433-2500; www.ethelm.com

Price: Free

The legendary chocolatier of M&Ms and Mars bars fame opens her factory about 10 miles southeast of the Strip to tourists who can see how the treats are made and packaged. Monitors explain the step-by-step process; when guests exit the tour, they step into a cactus garden full of ocotillo, prickly pear, and other desert delights. What's especially interesting about it is that the factory uses its waste water—32,000 gallons a day—for irrigating its landscaping, making it a longtime corporate model in this drought-stricken valley. More important to chocoholics, though, is the fact that every visitor gets a free chocolate.

Fremont Street Experience

425 Fremont St.

702/678-5777, www.vegasexperience.com

Price: Free

Shows are at the top of the hour, from nightfall until midnight.

Yes, it's downtown, which loses points with lots of Vegas-goers. But aside from Bellagio's fountains, the best free spectacle in town is the astonishingly clever light show projected onto the underside of a four-block-long metal canopy that arches over the Fremont Street pedestrian mall. In 2004, the Experience enjoyed a $17 million upgrade from 2.1 million incandescent bulbs to 12 million LEDs, making it, to date, the largest outdoor LED display in the world.

Hoover Dam

South on U.S. 93 to the Arizona border

866/291-8687; www.usbr.gov/lc/hooverdam

Price for museum: $11

In contrast to the Strip's glitz and glamour, Nevada's other wildly popular attraction, about 35 miles to the southeast, is a brainy tribute to architectural and scientific accomplishment. Built in the 1930s on the Colorado River at the Nevada-Arizona border, Hoover Dam stands 727 feet high, 1,244 feet long, and 660 feet thick at the base. The Discovery tour, which replaced the more impressive "hard-hat" tour that stopped after September 11, 2001, because of safety concerns, is nonetheless a fascinating look at how electricity is generated and how engineers used 3.2 million cubic yards of concrete to tame the mighty Colorado. Because the Southwest remains in the throes of its worst drought on record, visitors can easily notice that Lake Mead, formed by the dam, is more than 80 feet below its normal levels.

Lake Mead National Recreation Area

702/293-8990; www.nps.gov/lame/

Yes, it's a desert. But thanks to Hoover Dam, the largest man-made lake in North America is just a half-hour outside the Vegas Valley. It's perfect in warm weather for swimming, waterskiing, and boating, and many people rent houseboats for a weekend or a day to explore the 550 miles of shoreline. Among the vendors worth considering is Callville Bay Resort & Marina (800/255-5561; callvillebay.com), where you can rent a comfortable 44-foot patio pontoon for $275 a half-day or a bells-and-whistles 4-bedroom 70-foot houseboat complete with a spacious kitchen and a 36-inch TV for three days at $3,595.

Mount Charleston

702/515-5400; www.mtcharlestonlodge.com

Entrées at Lodge: $6-$45

Nothing surprises Vegas visitors more than finding out that a 12,000-foot mountain capped with snow seven months of the year is a mere 45-minute drive northwest of the hot desert city. Mount Charleston has long been a well-kept secret from dice-shooting tourists, a 316,000-acre alpine wonderland in the Humboldt-Toiyabe National Forest's Spring Mountain National Recreation Area. There are quaint cabins, ski slopes, and horseback riding areas; several tour operators offer hikes or drives through the area, which is typically 30 degrees cooler than the swelter of the Strip. The Mount Charleston Lodge restaurant serves up unimpressive German cuisine, but the views of the mountains make it tolerable. Rustic cabins are available for overnight stays at $125 and up per night.

Red Rock Canyon National Conservation Area

About 15 miles east of downtown Las Vegas on Charleston Blvd.

702/515-5367; www.redrockcanyonlv.org

Price: $5 per vehicle

Those 500-million-year-old looming red hills visible from most parts of Las Vegas Valley are a 15-minute drive west of, but worlds away from, the Strip. Local Las Vegans adore their most sensational bit of nature and bike, hike, or just drive through at any time of year. It's no wonder: Red Rock's 13-mile scenic route winds through a mountainous region that spans 130 square miles of Mojave Desert loaded with easy-to-spot Native American carvings, friendly wild burros, and places to rock climb. Guided hikes, of which there are dozens at varying levels of difficulty, are offered for almost every day in the spring and fall and leave from the visitor center. The high point on the scenic drive is an overlook at 4,760 feet, from which visitors can see the entire valley, including, on extremely clear days, the Strip.

Valley of Fire State Park

North of Las Vegas, about 10 miles east of the U.S. 169 exit in Interstate 15
702/397-2088; http://parks.nv.gov/vf.htm
Price: $6 per vehicle

There's no need to go all the way to Sedona, Arizona, for stunning beet-colored rock formations. About 45 minutes northwest of the Strip, the blank tumbleweed-plagued desert gives way to a basin of looming red and white sandstone hills that spread for more than 30,000 acres and provide some of Nevada's most exquisite hiking. The formations—some look like outsized beehives, one like an elephant—were created some 150 million years ago; Native Americans who lived here a thousand years ago left behind petroglyphs. The park's two campsites fill

up on a first-come, first-served basis. Nevada's oldest state park (1936), Valley of Fire has a new visitor center, with displays on the geology, history, and recreational opportunities of the region.

TOUR COMPANIES

Vegas visitors are inundated with offers, coupons, and advertisements from tour operators and travel agents. Here are three choices vetted to ensure the staff is gay friendly and the experience is worth the cost.

A Answer on Travel (702/731-2114): Gay travel agent Terry Wilsey has been guiding GLBT folks to great Vegas vacations for more than two decades. Wilsey not only knows everybody and everything, he's also a tireless volunteer for pretty much every GLBT cause in Nevada.

Boulder City Outfitters (800/748-3702; www.bouldercityoutfitters.com): For kayaking or canoe riding down the swift Colorado River below the Hoover Dam, these folks are the ones who know what they're doing. Their all-day kayak trip costs $163 per person and includes an expert guide who points out various caves and canyons of historical or geological interest. A free shuttle picks you up and returns you to your hotel.

Pink Jeep Tours (888/900-4480; www.pinkjeeptours.com): Yes, it sounds gay, but it's actually just a really solid tour company that drives you in hot pink vans or jeeps to Red Rock Canyon ($89), the Grand Canyon ($209), Hoover Dam ($79), and other points of regional interest.

Sundance Helicopters (At McCarran International Airport, 5596 Haven St., 702/736-0606; www.helicoptour.com): From a whirl around Vegas ($75 per person) with champagne to a flight to the rim of the Grand Canyon for a barbecue lunch ($335 pp), Sundance knows how to make quick comfortable work out of showing off the desert's splendor. Plus, they're very gay-friendly and happily invite gay couples to partake in their wedding packages.

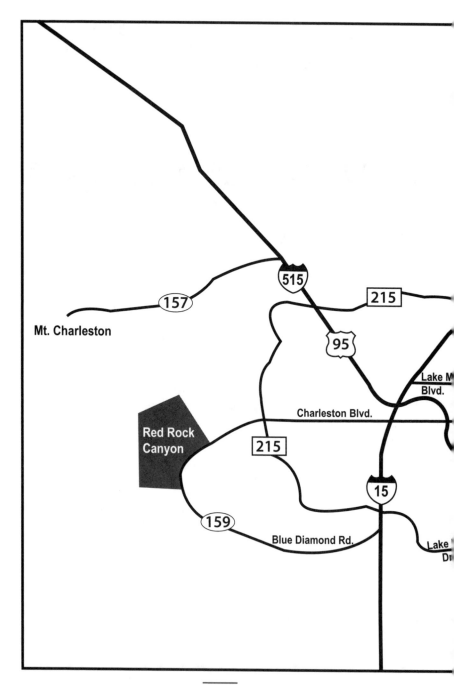

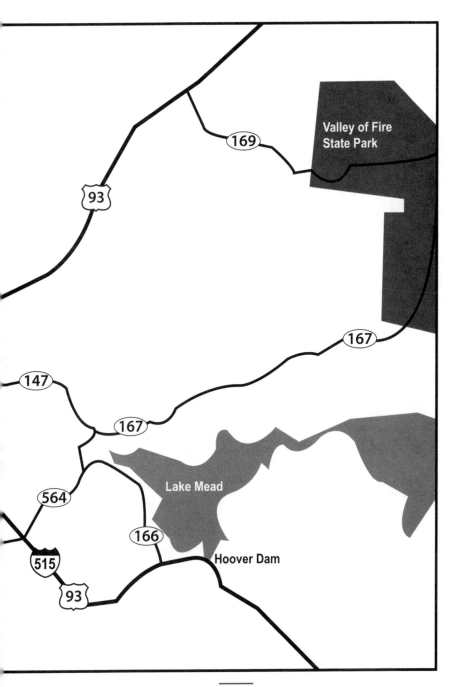

COMMUNITY 13

A. GLBT AND HIV/AIDS ORGANIZATIONS

ACLU of Nevada (702/366-1226; www.aclunv.org): Gay-friendly legal organization that offers legal advice and sues on behalf of those who believe their civil rights have been violated.

Affirmation (4640 Paradise Rd. #15-111, 702/647-3018; www.affirmation.org): GLBT Mormon prayer and support group.

Aid For AIDS of Nevada (AFAN) (2300 S. Rancho Dr. Suite 211, 702/382-2326; www. afanlv.org): A wide range of HIV/AIDS support services with an annual $1 million budget. Offers case management, financial assistance, legal support, food pantry, and an HIV-positive speakers bureau.

Alcoholics Together: A GLBT-focused Alcoholics Anonymous group. Meetings are daily at 12:15 p.m. and 8 p.m. Location is not published, so call 702/737-0035.

American Catholic Church (702/593-5395; www.american catholicchurch.net): A federation of independent churches offering a progressive alternative in the Catholic tradition. Catholic Mass is Saturday at 6:30 p.m. at Christ Episcopal Church, 2000 S. Maryland Parkway.

Betty's Outrageous Adventures (702/991-9929; www.bettysout. com): Lesbian hiking and outdoor-activity club.

Blackjack Bears of Las Vegas (702/225-4513; www.blackjackbears. org): A nonprofit social club for bears and their admirers that holds fundraisers for local charities.

Buddies Together (702/227-1599): Support groups for gay men over 40.

Caminar/Pedrigal House (702/471-6360; www.caminarinc.org): A charity that provides homes for indigent people with HIV/AIDS, both in terms of short-term rent assistance and with the 12-bedroom six-bath Pedrigal House for poor PWAs funded by Clark County and the U.S. Department of Housing and Urban Development.

The Center (953 E. Sahara Ave., 702/733-9800; www.thecenterlv .com): A full-service GLBT community hub with a $200,000 annual budget. Activities and support groups available for a wide spectrum of community members, such as teen and senior groups. Free anonymous HIV/AIDS and syphilis tests and free hepatitis A and B inoculations every Thursday 3–6:30 p.m.

Christ Episcopal Church (2000 S. Maryland Pkwy., 702/735-7655; www.christepiscopal.net): Episcopal Church with significant GLBT outreach, which hosts Gay Men's Chorus concerts and AA meetings.

Clark County Health District Office of AIDS (Ravenholt Public Health Center, 625 Shadow Lane Annex A, 702/759-0743; www.cchd. org/aids_prevention.htm): Offers HIV counseling and testing, partner counseling, outreach and community referrals, and safer-sex information distribution. Open Mon.-Fri. 8 a.m.–4 p.m.

Community Counseling Center (1140 Almond Tree Lane Suite 207, 702/369-8700; www.ccclasvegas.com): Founded by gay psychologist Ron Lawrence, the CCC is a counseling center that caters to low-income clients that also runs gay-specific support groups, HIV/AIDS counseling, and drug-addiction therapy.

Delta Lambda Phi (702/896-8110; www.dlp.org/mu): A gay fraternity with a chapter at the University of Nevada-Las Vegas. Membership is open to non-students.

Desert Brotherhood Motorcycle Club (702/456-7661): A social club for GLBT motorcycle enthusiasts, with regular rides and events at the Buffalo Bar.

Foster Care and Adoption Association of Nevada (702/657-6470): An organization of foster and adoptive parents, including GLBT parents, who work together on issues related to at-risk children.

Fun One Bowling (www.funones.net): Gay and lesbian bowling league that meets on 11:30 a.m. on Sundays at the Gold Coast Hotel-Casino's bowling center, 4000 W. Flamingo Road.

Gay and Lesbian Financial Club (702/310-5048; www.thecenterlv.com): Social group for GLBT people interested in finance and investing. Meets 7 p.m. on the third Wednesday of the month at the Center, 953 E. Sahara Avenue.

Gay & Lesbian Book Discussion Club (702/733-9800; www.thecenterlv.com): Reading club that meets at 7:30 p.m. on the third Monday of each month at the Center, 953 E. Sahara Avenue.

Gay Science Fiction Club (702/380-8605; www.thecenterlv.com): Group of sci-fi fans gather at 7:30 p.m. on the fourth Monday of the month at the Center, 953 E. Sahara Avenue.

Gay Switchboard of Las Vegas (702/733-9990): Gay hotline for free travel and local-services information.

Gay, Lesbian and Straight Educators Network of Southern Nevada (702/371-1351): Group that offers help and advocacy on behalf of GLBT teachers and students. The organization also keeps track of all the gay-straight alliances at Southern Nevada high schools.

G-Men Discussion Group (702/733-9800; www.thecenterlv.com): Support group for gay men that meets every Friday at 7 p.m. at the Center, 953 E. Sahara Avenue.

Golden Rainbow (702/384-2899; www.goldenrainbow.org): Provides housing for people with HIV/AIDS.

Human Rights Campaign (HRC-LasVegas@cox.net): Political-action committee that lobbies for GLBT rights and in support of GLBT-supportive candidates. Holds socials on the third Thursday of the month at various restaurants.

Imago Dei Las Vegas (336 Cathedral Way, 702/354-2294; www.imagodeilv.org): Catholic ministry by and for GLBT of faith and their friends with several events each month.

Imperial Royal Sovereign Court of the Desert Empire, Inc. (www.desertempire.org): A non-profit group that holds drag shows and contests and has raised more than $100,000 for other charities in Vegas.

Lambda Business & Professional Association (702/593-2875; www.lambdalv.com): GLBT professional and business association providing an atmosphere of success through networking, support, and education. Members sign a code of ethics. Holds monthly luncheons at 11:30 a.m. on the second Wednesday of the month at various locations.

Las Vegas Men's Chorus (702/453-5862): A gay chorus that usually puts on two concerts a year, one around June and another at Christmastime. The schedule has been erratic in recent years.

Las Vegas Prime Timers (www.lasvegasprimetimers.com): A social group for older gay and bisexual men. Holds group chats, dinners, and recreational activities several times a month.

Las Vegas Sunrunners (702/363-6862): Nudist group. Several events each month and an active list-serv at groups.yahoo.com/group/LVSunrunners.

Leather Uniform Club of Las Vegas (702/362-1485; www.lucoflv.com): Group for leather guys and their admirers. Meets at 7:30 p.m. on the second Wednesday of the month at the Las Vegas Eagle, 3430 E. Tropicana Avenue.

L-Group (702/733-9800; www.thecenterlv.com): A lesbian support and social group. Meets at 7 p.m. Fridays at the Center, 953 E. Sahara Avenue.

Metropolitan Community Church of Las Vegas (1140 Almond Tree Lane, 702/369-4380; www.mcclv.com): Nondenominational Christian church for GLBTs and supporters. Services are 10 a.m. on Sunday. Bible study is at 6 p.m. on Wednesdays.

Narcotics Anonymous (900 E. Karen Ste. 202, 702/362-1485): Gay-centric meetings of the substance-abuse support group meet at this address. The phone number doubles as a 24-hour hotline.

National Lesbian and Gay Journalists Association, Las Vegas (702/384-1435; www.nlgja.org): Professional association for GLBT journalists, educators, and media professionals. Runs annual Excellence in Journalism contest.

Neon Fest (www.neonfest.org): The organization behind the annual GLBT film festival and sporadic film screenings.

Neon Squares (702/524-8390): GLBT square-dance club.

Nevada AIDS Project (702/636-1000; www.nevadaaidsproject. org): A newer HIV/AIDS services organization that seems to focus mainly on support-group programs. The group also operates and benefits from Artspace Gallery, 1400 S. Third St., an art, furniture, and antique gallery in downtown Las Vegas next to the gay bar Snick's Place.

Nevada Gay Rodeo Association (www.ngra.com): An all-volunteer non-profit organization that puts on the Big Horn Rodeo in Las Vegas in October and raises money for local GLBT charities.

Nevada Outdoors (702/860-7110; www.nevadaoutdoors.org): An active group that organizes frequent hikes in the Vegas-area mountains, has monthly dinners, and goes on occasional campouts in Nevada, Arizona, and Utah. Meets 7 p.m. on the last Wednesday of the month at the Center, 953. E Sahara Avenue.

Parents and Friends of Lesbians and Gays (702/438-7838): Support and advocacy group for parents and friends of GLBT people.

Por Amour Couples (702/731-2114): Gay and lesbian couples gather the last Saturday of the month for a potluck dinner in the homes of a member couple.

Progressive Leadership Alliance of Nevada (702/791-1965; www.planevada.org): A statewide liberal political group that considers GLBT rights as part of its aim.

Saint Therese Center (67 E. Lake Mead Dr., Henderson, 702/564-4224; www.sainttheresecenter.org): An HIV/AIDS support agency that provides food and other assistance to indigent people with HIV/AIDS.

Senior Social Connections (702/733-9800; www.thecenterlv.com): A social and support group for GLBT senior citizens that meets at 2 p.m. on the second Sunday of each month.

Sin City Q Socials (www.sincityqsocials.com): A social group for GLBT business professionals that meets for drinks at various bars at 8 p.m. every Tuesday.

Southern Nevada Association of Pride, Inc. (702/615-9429; www.lasvegaspride.org): The non-profit organization that puts on the annual gay pride festivals each May. Profits are donated to other local GLBT charities.

Sin City Chamber of Commerce (5852 S. Pecos, Rd. Ste. H-8, 702/450-7222;

www.sincitychamberofcommerce.com): A chamber of commerce for GLBT, sin, and other businesses, with events that include an annual barbecue at a brothel.

Sin Sity Sisters (702/591-6969; www.sinsitysisters.org): A chapter of the Sisters of Perpetual Indulgence, that group of drag queens in outlandish nun attire who perform to raise money for various gay and HIV/AIDS charities. See site for upcoming events.

Spectrum (702/594-4297; www.unlv.edu/student_orgs/spectrum): The GLBT student group at the University of Nevada-Las Vegas.

Stonewall Democratic Club (702/214-3610; www.stonewalllv.org): A gay-Democrats organization that holds monthly meetings and such events as coffees with politicians and voter-registration drives.

Transgender Support and Advocacy Nevada (4343 N. Rancho Dr. #234, 702/392-2132; Tsanevada@aol.com): Support and political group for transgender people.

University Medical Center HIV Wellness Center (2300 S. Rancho Dr. Ste. 205, 702/383-2691; www.umc-cares.org/med_serv/hiv): Outpatient services, dental care, clinical trials for people with HIV/AIDS. Treatment offered on a sliding-scale payment program. Hours Mon.–Fri. 7 a.m.–5 p.m.

Unitarian Universalist Congregation of Las Vegas (3616 E. Lake Mead Blvd., 702/437-2404; www.uuclv.org): A pro-gay Christian denomination.

Valley Outreach Synagogue (702/436-4900; www.valleyoutreach synagogue.com): A reconstructionist Jewish synagogue that is very welcoming to GLBT congregants. Services held at 7:30 p.m. the first Friday of each month at the Oasis Christian Church, Sun City Mac-Donald Ranch Community Center, 10450 Gilespie Street.

Vegas Chubby Chasers (www.vegaschubbychasers.com): Group for heavy-set gays and those who love them. Holds a party from 10 p.m. to 2 a.m. every third Saturday of the month at the Eagle, 3430 E. Tropicana Avenue.

Vegas MPowerment (702/733-9800; www.thecenterlv.com): Bisexual and gay men's support group. Meets 7 p.m. on Mondays, Wednesdays, and Fridays at the Center.

We Are Family LV (www.wearefamilylv.com): A support and social group for GLBT people with children.

Wise Womyn (702/369-4380): Support group for mature lesbians at the Metropolitan Community Church meets noon–1 p.m. on Wednesdays.

Women of Diversity (702/655-2146; www.womenofdiversity.org): A non-profit group that encourages visibility and inclusion of women of all types, including lesbians, in film, books, and other media.

Youth Sensations (702/733-9800): Gay and lesbian youth support group, which meets at 6–8 p.m. on Thursdays at the Center, 953 E. Sahara Avenue.

Q & A with Candice Nichols

Longtime activist Candice Nichols didn't come out until she'd been through two straight divorces and had turned 38. Since then, however, she's been one of the city's most outspoken lesbians in a town with precious few outspoken lesbians. The Las Vegas native, always a left-wing advocate, spent more than a decade working for Planned Parenthood and Aid for AIDS in Nevada (AFAN) before landing in 2004 the job as executive director of the Center, a 4,500-square-foot GLBT facility founded in 1993.

Q: What took you so long to come out?

A: I didn't know where the lesbians were. I didn't know where to find the community. I got married very young and then divorced and I really wanted to come out in my early 20s, but then I couldn't figure out how to find a woman, how to know who was a lesbian. So I got married again, this time as an open bisexual woman, and we had two children. It lasted 16 years.

Q: How has the community progressed?

A: We're still in our infancy compared to a lot of other cities that have had a GLBT center for 20 or 30 years. We've only been around since 1993. But there are larger cities than ours that don't have centers, so we're not doing that badly.

Q: There's lots of stuff for gay men here. Where are the lesbians?

A: It's really funny, but the women here say they want something like Girlbar (the lesbian night at Krāve), but when they get it, they don't support it. Then again, the drinks at Girlbar are like $10 each. With those prices, who can afford it? Women don't have the same disposable money that gay men do. We're paid less.

Q: There are lots of lesbians out at Free Zone and Flex and those bars. Are gay men and lesbians better integrated here?

A: Yeah. When we had our Christmas party, we had some gay men from Los Angeles visiting and they were so pleased to see the women at this event. Back in L.A., they said, you'd never see that. It's more of a separatist community in other places.

Q: Do the needs The Center responds to tend to revolve around the young and old?

A: Yes, because they're disenfranchised by the broader gay community. When you have a culture of beautiful men and bodies and muscles, the older men don't fit into those categories and they're ignored. And the young are disenfranchised because they can't go into the bars and that kind of thing. But they come here so they can all be gay together. Gives them have a sense of community.

Q: How is the community in terms of AIDS services and support?

A: If you're broke and indigent, they're great. Otherwise, not so good.

Q: What problems do the GLBT community in Las Vegas face?

A: Oh, the same as everywhere else—gay marriage, adoption, we're all still looking for basic civil rights that are not always afforded to us. We're going to be fighting for that for a while.

(B) ANNUAL GAY EVENTS

FEBRUARY:

• **NGRA Board of Directors Annual Show** (702/615-6261; www.ngra.com): An evening of gay performances at Badlands Saloon to benefit the Nevada Gay Rodeo Association. Typically includes a beer bust and raffle.

• **Naked Hearts** (www.goldenrainbow.org): A Valentine's Day revue at Krāve benefiting Golden Rainbow featuring cast members of several Strip shows, typically including folks from *Chippendales, Mamma Mia!,* and *La Cage.* Also features a kissing booth and aerialists.

APRIL:

• **AIDS Walk** (702/382-2326; www.afanlv.org): The annual walk raises funds for Aid For AIDS in Nevada, the region's largest HIV/AIDS support-services agency. The course usually runs around downtown Las Vegas.

• **Chicken Ranch BBQ** (www.sincitychamberofcommerce. com): An annual cookout for members of the Sin City Chamber of Commerce at the famed Chicken Ranch brothel in Pahrump, about 60 miles outside Las Vegas.

• **Bear Hunt** (www.blackjackbears.org): An annual convention for more than 200 big hairy guys and their admirers. Events include the

Bear Hug at the Apollo bathhouse, the Steak Fry, the Disco Bear Boxer Beer Bust at the Eagle, and the Bare Bear Buns Contest. See Web site for up-to-date information.

• **SmokeOUT**: A four-day weekend of parties and events for gay men who love cigars, pipes, and all things tobacco, hosted by the Desert Brotherhood Motorcycle Club. See www.bearland.com/intro. htm or join a list-serv providing updated information and discussion at groups.yahoo.com/group/las-vegas-smokeout.

• **Dining Out For Life** (www.diningoutforlife.com): A citywide AIDS benefit in which on one April night of the year, participating restaurants donate a portion of their revenues to the Saint Therese Center.

• **Queer Prom**: A dance and social organized by the Gay and Lesbian Center of Southern Nevada youth coordinator Joshua Montgomery and hosted by the Christ Episcopal Church (2100 S. Maryland Pkwy.) for anyone ages 13-24 interested in attending. The 2006 dance, the fourth annual, drew more than 120 attendees. Usually the last Saturday of April from 7-11 p.m., that may change from year to year so call 702/733-9800 or visit www.thecenterlv.com to inquire.

MAY:

• **Art Auction** (702/733-9800; www.thecenterlv.com): One week before Pride, the Center hosts an art auction in which they sell the donated works of local artists.

• **Pride Royalty Pageant** (702/615-9429; www.lasvegaspride. org): The Southern Nevada Association of Pride Inc., which puts on the annual gay-pride festival, hosts this yearly event to crown various honoraries for the event. Titles bestowed are Mr. Las Vegas Pride, Miss Las Vegas Pride, Miss At Large Las Vegas Pride, Miss Transsexual Las Vegas Pride, and Ms. Las Vegas Pride. Contestants must be Vegas residents over 21.

• **Las Vegas GLBT Pride Week** (www.lasvegaspride.org): Typically includes the nation's only nighttime GLBT Pride parade, in downtown Las Vegas, followed by an all-day festival and fair at a local park. There are also men's and women's events at various clubs. See Web site for updates.

JUNE:

• **Big Bash Sin City** (www.bigguyevents.com): A three-day weekend of parties and events for fat gay men and their admirers. Usually hosted by the Blue Moon Resort.

• **Ribbon of Life show** (www.goldenrainbow.org): A major benefit revue featuring hundreds of dancers, singers, and actors from Strip shows and UNLV arts groups. There are two performances and a silent auction. The money raised, typically more than $200,000 a year, supports Golden Rainbow, which provides housing assistance for people with HIV/AIDS.

- **Out on the Strip** (www.nlgja.org): A fundraiser to benefit the Las Vegas chapter of the National Lesbian and Gay Journalists Association and present results of the annual NLGJA-LV Excellence in Journalism contest.

JULY:

- **Aunt Betty's Annual Chili Cook-Off** (www.goldenrainbow.org): A chili cook-off that raises money for local food pantries and Golden Rainbow, which provides housing for people with HIV/AIDS. The event includes a contest for best chili and cornbread and worst chili and a silent auction.

- **Toddy Awards show** (www.goldenrainbow.org): A midnight awards ceremony typically held at Krāve that honors the best of the performers and performances in the Golden Rainbow benefit show each June. No cover charge, but donations are encouraged.

SEPTEMBER:

- **Big Horn Rodeo** (www.bighornrodeo.com): The gay rodeo put on by the Nevada Gay Rodeo Association typically attracts thousands. This is the first event on the International Gay Rodeo Association's annual calendar. Includes bareback bronc riding, bull riding, pole bending, calf roping, and several other rodeo events. The event benefits St. Therese Center and Santa Saturday West. And takes place at Horsemans Park. Gets proclamations from the governor, mayor, and Congress. Well, Democrats, anyway. Sometimes is held in October, so check Web site for updates.

- **Black and White Party** (702/382-2326; www.afanlv.org): An annual food and drink festival at a major Strip hotel-casino where folks

are encouraged to bring canned goods and wear black and white. The event raises more than $80,000 a year for Aid For AIDS in Nevada, the largest HIV/AIDS support-services agency. Sometimes takes place in late August, so see Web site for updates.

• **HRC Gala Dinner:** The local Human Rights Campaign holds this fundraising dinner with pretty high-profile guests of honor. In 2006, for instance, they included U.S. Senator Harry Reid.

OCTOBER:

• **Beaux Arts Ball** (www.goldenrainbow.org): A Halloween costume bash at the MGM Grand's Studio 54 to benefit Golden Rainbow, featuring performances by cast members of various Strip shows.

• **Circle of Roses** (www.sainttheresecenter.org): A fundraising dinner for the Saint Therese Center.

• **Lucky Bear Weekend** (www.luckybearweekend.com): A social gathering of bears and their fans for a weekend of parties, shows, and other activities. Usually takes place at the Blue Moon Resort.

• **National Coming-Out-Day Street Fair** (www.ncodvegas.com): Three days of parties and events include a mammoth street fair in the Fruit Loop area sponsored by *QVegas* in honor of National Coming-Out Day.

- **Neon Fest** (www.neonfest.org): Three-day GLBT film festival.

NOVEMBER:

- **Honorarium** (702/733-9800; www.the centerlv.com): The major fundraiser for the Center is this awards ceremony for GLBT leaders and community members who have made a difference. There's usually a prominent national speaker like U.S. Rep. Barney Frank, and straight allies are also feted.

DECEMBER:

- **AFAN Kids' Holiday Party** (702/382-2326; www.afanlv.org): Aid for AIDS of Nevada hosts a party for the children affected by HIV/AIDS in Clark County. The group raises money for gingerbread-cookie decorating and toys for the kids.

- **Christmas Tree and Wreath Auction** (702/733-9800; www.thecenterlv.com): The Center hosts this auction, in which they sell donated decorated trees and wreaths as a benefit.

- **Coronation** (www.desertempire.org): The Imperial Royal Sovereign Court of the Desert Empire holds a weekend-long event to crown the following year's emperor, empress, imperial crown prince royale, and imperial crown princess royale.

- **Krāve Kares** (www.kravelasvegas.com): An annual fundraiser at the Krāve nightclub in which patrons are encouraged to bring donations of cash and essential items (i.e. backpacks and clothes) for the Nevada Partnership for Homeless Youth. The nightclub donates the cover charge for the night.

SEX AND THE (SIN) CITY

A. BATHHOUSES

Apollo Spa and Health Club (953 E. Sahara Ave. A19, 702/650-9191; www.apollospa.com): Located in the northwest-most corner of the Commercial Center complex on Sahara Avenue, by most accounts, the Apollo is a reliable but very badly kept and expensive bathhouse that reeks of mildew. Non-members $25 locker or $30 room fee. Open 24 hours.

Hawks Gym (953 E. Sahara Ave., Building 35 Ste. 102, 702/731-4295; www.hawksgymlv.com): With the Apollo in long-term disrepair, this spot is its popular heir apparent and, since it's also in the Commercial Center, is a neighbor in the southeast corner. It's gay-owned, unlike Apollo. Its major innovation is a 1,200-foot dungeon complete with a seven-foot spider web of chain and that all-important spanking bench. There's also an aerobics and meditation room, though it's unclear how much that or the actual gym equipment gets used. $7 for day membership, $13 for locker and towel, $23 for room. $15 for 3-month membership. Cash only. Busiest times are 11 p.m.–5 a.m. on Friday and Saturdays.

B. BOOKSTORES

A-Action Adult Books & Videos (1016 S. 1st St., 702/382-1076): Run! Yikes! It's a tough call which is scarier, the broken-down interior with an arcade lacking doors to the stalls or the outside, where your car is likely to be stolen if you're not mugged first. Do not go here without your own transportation. A quarter gets you into the joint.

Adult Superstore (1147 Las Vegas Blvd. S., 702/383-8326): This adult video arcade is about two miles north of the Sahara Hotel-Casino on Las Vegas Boulevard. It's basically clean, although the area's not especially safe at night. $1 minimum in arcade; $8 for viewing movies.

Adult World (3781 Meade Ave., 702/579-9736): This porn and sex-toys shop with video arcade is about two miles west of north end of the Strip. $3 card required for entry to arcade area. Open 24/7.

Fantasy World (6760 Boulder Hwy., 702/433-6311): A very clean, large, adult video store a bit off the beaten path that may be good for folks coming or going from Hoover Dam. $5 credit required to enter arcade; $8 for private room to watch a DVD of your choice. Open 24/7.

Industrial Books (3427 Industrial Rd., 702/734-7667): While this adult porn shop is walking distance from the Mirage and Wynn and is directly behind the Fashion Show Mall, it's still poorly kept and has a very scummy feel to it. $3 card required for arcade entry. Gross. Open 24/7.

The Rack (953 E. Sahara in Commercial Center, 702/732-7225): The Rack sells sex toys and has a new porn theater called Onyx. Particularly in the Onyx area, there's heavy cruising in the store. Open 24/7.

Wild J's Book and Video (2915 Industrial Rd., 702/892-0699): If the choice is between Industrial Books and here, this one is much cleaner and more pleasant. It's directly behind Circus Circus with a bright purple sign out front. $3 credit required to enter arcade; $8 for private room to watch a DVD of your choice.

C. CRUISING

The following is a list of reputed areas in Las Vegas where active gay cruising going on. Please note that public sex or lewdity is not legal in Nevada and engaging in sexual activity in any of these locations could result in arrest. Several Web sites, including cruisingforsex.com, provide the up-to-the-minute status of various locations.

24-Hour Fitness at McCarran Airport: Located near the baggage claim area in McCarran Airport, enter via elevator on the second floor near the post office above the south baggage area. The cruisy locker room is popular among flight attendants and TSA workers. Open all hours, except closes at midnight Friday and Saturday and reopens at 6 a.m.

Blue Moon Resort (2651 Westwood Dr., 702/361-9099; www.bluemoonlv.com): For heavy sexual activity, this is the place (see page 55). The entire property is clothing-optional. There's a very nice pool area with waterfall and steam room. $20 day passes for non-guests, who can stay until 7 p.m.

Boulevard Mall (3528 S. Maryland Pkwy.): Find cruisy toilets downstairs in Macy's near men's shoes and near food court.

Caesars Palace (702/731-7776): The health club on the second floor of the Palace Tower is cruisy. Open 6 a.m.–8 p.m. $30 non-guest day pass.

Luxor (702/730-5720): Nurture was once known as a very cruisy health club, but the action's simmered some since it stopped being a 24-hour facility. Still, its reputation continues to lure seekers. Open 6 a.m.–8 p.m. $25 non-guest day pass.

Las Vegas Hilton (702/732-5648): Cruising is common at the health club, which is open 6 a.m.–8 p.m. Steam Room closes at 7:30 p.m. $20 day pass for guests or non-guests.

Spa Mandalay (877/632-7300): A neighbor of Luxor and oft-dubbed Mandalay Gay for its heavy queer quotient, the 30,000-square-foot spa is known as very popular. Late afternoon is said to be especially active. (Note: Despite the provocative name, the Bathhouse Spa at the other Mandalay Bay tower, THEhotel at Mandalay, is not known for gay cruising.) Open 6 a.m.–8:30 p.m. $27 for guests, $30 non-guest day pass.

McCarran International Airport: The parking lot of the viewing area, which is off Sunset between Las Vegas Blvd. and Eastern, is known to be a pick-up spot. Also, the toilet near gates B14 to B18 to the left of the Fox Sports Bar is cruisy.

MGM Grand Hotel (702/891-3077): The toilet in the Studio Walk near the Coyote Café is known to be cruisy late at night. Also, some activity is reported at the health club. Spa hours: 6 a.m.–8 p.m. $25 day rate for hotel guests only. Non-guests not allowed.

Mirage: Another cruisy hotel-casino spa. Non-guests allowed to buy $20 day passes on Mondays through Thursdays only, although non-guests staying at other MGM Mirage properties are exempt from that restriction. Open 6 a.m.–7 p.m. Guest day passes are also $20.

Sunset Park (2601 E. Sunset Rd.): The cruisy parking lot is located at Eastern Avenue near Warm Springs Road, southwest of McCarran International Airport.

University of Nevada-Las Vegas campus: Located along Maryland Parkway between Flamingo Road and Tropicana Avenue. There's a cruisy locker room at the Paul McDermott Physical Education center (MPE), particularly in the late afternoons. Also, try the toilets in the basement of the Flora Dungan Humanities building and on the first floor of the Beam College of Business.

D. NUDIST SPOTS

Au Natural Nudist Colony (5150 Los Piños St., 702/731-6935; www.aunaturallv.com): Out in the southeast corner of the Las Vegas Valley is an oasis for nudists that the straight owner, Ty, says he hopes will become a "United Nations of alternative lifestyles." Ty and his girlfriend, Brianna, took over this surprisingly nice two-acre spread in 2005 from relatives of Brianna, whose grandmother owns the notorious Red Rooster Swingers' Club next door. The nudist colony comprises four modular homes, each with three bedrooms, as well as a well-kept outdoor swimming pool, a Jacuzzi, gym, and DVD library. Since guest homes and B&Bs are illegal in Las Vegas, Ty and Brianna say they "ask" for a $70 "donation" for a small room and a $100 "donation" for a larger one. They have regular parties and say they're planning to host weekly gay events. $10 per person for a day pass.

Lake Mead National Recreation Area's Gay/Nude Beach: An uncomfortable section of the rocky and prickly shoreline of Lake Mead has been claimed by gay men as the region's "gay/nude" beach. Still, public nudity and sexual activity in public are illegal in Nevada and park rangers occasionally—though rarely—check on the area. To get there, take I-15 to Lake Mead Blvd., which is north of the Strip, not to be mistaken for Lake Mead Drive, which is south of the Strip. Go east past Hollywood Blvd. and past the park entrance gate. Proceed for several miles until you come to a stop sign. Turn left and head north toward Overton. Set your odometer and drive 4.8 miles, then go right onto the gravel 8.0 Road. Park in the lot overlooking the lake and hike north for five minutes into a little ravine and over a hill along a narrow trail. The beach is active in summer months. $5 park gate fee per vehicle for the Lake Mead Recreation Area.

INDEX

INDEX

INDEX

ABOUT THE AUTHOR

 Freelance writer Steve Friess first moved to Las Vegas in 1996 to work for the *Las Vegas Review-Journal.* A former contributing writer for *The Advocate,* Friess has also covered gay topics for *USA Today,* the *New York Times, Newsweek,* and dozens of other major periodicals. The Long Island native also founded the Las Vegas chapter of the National Lesbian and Gay Journalists Association and is a former NLGJA board member. Friess and his partner, NBC producer Miles Smith, co-host "The Strip" podcast, a weekly Vegas-centric celebrity-interview program found at TheStripPodcast.com. Friess and Smith wed at the Palms Hotel-Casino in March 2007 and live with their two Chihuahuas, Black and Jack. He can be reached at www.stevefriess.com and he welcomes any and all feedback.